ACHIEVING
EYPS

Working with Parents in Early Years Settings

Ute Ward

Series editors: Lyn Trodd and Gill Goodliff

LearningMatters

British Library Cataloguing in Publication Data
A CIP record for this book is available from the British Library.

ISBN: 978 1 84445 268 2

Text design by Code 5 Design Associates Ltd
Cover design by Phil Barker
Project management by Swales and Willis
Typeset by Swales and Willis
Printed and bound in Great Britain by TJ International Ltd, Padstow, Cornwall

Learning Matters Ltd
33 Southernhay East
Exeter EX1 1NX
Tel: 01392 215560
info@learningmatters.co.uk
www.learningmatters.co.uk

Dedication

For my parents

Für meine Eltern

Contents

Foreword from the series editors

This book is one of a series which will be of interest to all those following pathways towards achieving Early Years Professional Status (EYPS). This includes students on Sector-Endorsed Foundation Degree in Early Years programmes and undergraduate Early Childhood Studies degree courses as these awards are key routes towards EYPS.

The graduate EYP role was created as a key strategy in government commitment to improve the quality of Early Years care and education in England, especially in the private, voluntary and independent sectors. Policy documents and legislation such as *Every Child Matters: Change for Children*, DfES (2004); the *Ten Year Childcare Strategy: Choice for Parents – the Best Start for Children* HMT (2004), and the Childcare Act, 2006, identified the need for high-quality, well-trained and educated professionals to work with the youngest children. The government's aim – restated in the 2020 Children and Young People's Workforce Strategy (DCSF, 2008) – is to have an Early Years Professional (EYP) in all children's centres by 2010 and in every full day care setting by 2015, with two graduates in disadvantaged areas.

This book is distinctive in the series in that its particular focus is on children in the context of their families. The reader is left in no doubt of the author's commitment to working with parents in her own practice. The book acknowledges the parent as the child's first teacher and explores how positive relationships can be developed between parents and practitioners through the work of the Early Years Professional. Ute Ward has taken into account new initiatives such as the National Academy for Parenting Practitioners as well as drawing on established authorities on the subject of 'Working with Parents'. Her intention is to challenge the reader to reflect on his or her attitudes towards parents and to gain essential self-knowledge, understanding and inter-personal skills.

The reader will find helpful links made to other key responsibilities for Early Years Professionals such as how to support transition and to take into account the context of the local community. Case studies and self-assessment questions are used to focus on the practice of Early Years Professionals. This enables the reader to consider how to meet the EYP Standards in full by modelling excellent practice while promoting and encouraging it in colleagues.

Lyn Trodd and Gill Goodliff,
May 2009

About the author and series editors

Ute Ward

Ute Ward has been involved in the Early Years sector for the past 19 years as a parent, volunteer, play group assistant and play group leader. Recognising the vital role parents play in a child's life she moved to working more directly with adults first as a development officer and tutor for the Pre-school Learning Alliance and then for four years as Community Involvement Co-ordinator in a Sure Start Local Programme. In November 2007 Ute became manager of a phase 2 Children's Centre and is now also developing a phase 3 Children's Centre.

Lyn Trodd

Lyn Trodd is Head of Children's Workforce Development at the University of Hertfordshire. Lyn is the Chair of the National Network of Sector-Endorsed Foundation Degrees in Early Years. She was involved in the design of Early Years Professional Status and helped to pilot the Validation Pathway when it first became available. Lyn has published and edited a range of articles, national and international conference papers and books focusing on self-efficacy in the child and the practitioner and also the professional identity and role of adults who work with young children.

Gill Goodliff

Gill Goodliff is a Senior Lecturer and Head of Awards for Early Years at the Open University where she has developed and chaired courses on the Sector-Endorsed Foundation Degree and as a Lead Assessor for Early Years Professional Status. Her professional work with young children and their families was predominantly in the voluntary sector. Her research interests centre on the professional identities of early years practitioners and young children's spirituality.

Acknowledgements

My thanks go to my colleagues, past and present. I have learnt so much from them, and with them, that this book could not have been written without them. I am also grateful to Lyn Trodd for encouraging me and enabling me to write this book. But most of all I have to thank all the parents and children I have worked with over the years – they have been and still are a constant source of insight and inspiration.

Ute Ward,
May 2009

Introduction

Years ago I left the small village pre-school where I was working as play group leader because I felt very frustrated. Seeing most children for only two or three mornings a week I seemed to make little difference in their lives. I changed my career to focus on working with adults, initially as a pre-school development officer and then as tutor, thinking that my scope to enhance children's lives would be greater by working with parents in pre-school committees and with staff members. Several years of Sure Start Local Programme experience and hands-on parent involvement and community development work later I realise that it is not a question of working with *either* children *or* adults but a question of working with both, parents *and* children. This is the key to improving the well-being and learning of children. I know now that all those years ago I should not have left my pre-school; I should have stayed and started working differently and more intensively with the parents in addition to my work with their children.

This book is about the more intensive work with parents. It explores why it is important, how the relationship between Early Years practitioners and parents can be improved, and what the challenges are in this partnership. The book is of interest to any practitioner who works with parents and wants to extend her practice in this area. However, each chapter makes particular reference to the standards required for the Early Years Professional Status making the book a valuable resource for undergraduate and post-graduate students of Early Years and childhood studies. Although the focus for this book is very strongly on the adults in a child's life, and children often do not get mentioned for several pages, it does not mean that the child is not important. The whole purpose of the partnership between professional and parent is the well-being, learning and development of the child. The details of how you can work effectively with children are, however, explored elsewhere. Here the parent is at the centre of attention so that you can explore how you can change your way of working with parents to engage them deeply in their children's learning while also addressing their learning and development together with your own.

The first three chapters in this book will examine your attitudes to parents and your approach to working in partnership with them. Chapter 1 explores the enduring contribution parents make to their children's lives. Chapter 2 focusses on assumptions and prejudices towards parents and families and outlines some values and beliefs which support effective partnership working between professionals and parents. Chapter 3 examines the relationships between parents, children and professionals in more detail. Chapters 4, 5 and 7 will lead you to exploring the different practical aspects of parental engagement and involvement, especially with parents described as 'hard-to-reach'. Chapter 6 is dedicated to adult learning, and Chapter 8 outlines the link between partnership working in Early Years settings and community development work. The emphasis throughout the book is twofold: on the one hand it draws a link between research and theory and daily work and on the other it aims to stimulate reflection and discussion leading to improvements in practice. The reflective and practical tasks in each chapter help you to explore your own practice but can also be used to stimulate discussion in your setting or staff team. Furthermore, you will find two or three self-assessment questions at the end of each chapter which are designed to enforce some of the key learning points. Many of the examples, research papers and case studies refer to pre-schools, Sure Start Local Programmes and children's centres but are just as relevant to day nurseries or nursery classes. The term 'Early Years setting' which I use throughout the book is deliberately wide because many of the principles and practices discussed apply regardless of the exact environment you work in. Where I use the term 'Early Years practitioner' I include all staff members working in an Early Years setting, while the term 'Early Years Professional' refers to a staff member in a leading role with responsibility for shaping practice and managing a staff team. With the terms 'child' and 'parent' I alternate between masculine and feminine pronouns to avoid the dominance of one gender over the other. On occasions, I write about 'your children' in which case I am referring to the children in your setting rather than your own children.

Depending on your experience and the context you work in, much of the contents of this book may already be familiar to you and the work with parents may seem quite simple and easy. Or many of the book's ideas and suggestions may be completely new to you and you feel overwhelmed by how difficult the work with parents appears. Working with parents is neither the one, nor the other; like all human interaction it is complex, at times demanding and challenging, and sometimes very frustrating, but it is also highly stimulating, occasionally very moving and often greatly rewarding. And most importantly, it makes a real difference to the children you work with.

1   The role of the parent in a child's life

CHAPTER OBJECTIVES

After reading this chapter you should be able to:
- analyse the contribution parents and the home environment make to children's well-being, development and learning;
- assess critically the benefits of parental involvement in Early Years settings for the child and for the parent;
- examine the inter-relatedness of parents' involvement, teachers' expectations and children's achievements.

This chapter begins to develop your knowledge and understanding of parental involvement and is particularly relevant to 'S3', 'S7', 'S29', 'S30', and 'S38'. These standards require you to reflect on the influence parents have on their child's development and on your approach to working with them to enhance their children's learning. You will explore what is meant by the term 'parents' and gain an understanding of the impact parents and their engagement in Early Years settings have on children. The chapter will consider how involvement in children's learning and Early Years settings affects parents themselves and enhances their lives and how this influences your work as an Early Years Professional.

Understanding the term 'parents'

Parents and the home environment they create are the single most important factor in shaping their children's well-being, achievements and prospects.

(Department for Education and Skills [DfES], 2007, p1)

In the document *Every Parent Matters* the Government sets out its vision for parents including an understanding of their roles, the support they may require at different times during their children's development and the commitment to action from Government Departments, Local Authorities and others. The crucial role of the parent in a child's life is clearly acknowledged and ways of supporting this role explored. There is a growing understanding, evidenced from research, that parents' views need to be heard more and taken into consideration more in the Early Years sector and throughout children's schooling (for example Desforges and Abouchaar, 2003, Siraj-Blatchford *et al*, 2002). To achieve this, parents will have to have the opportunity to engage actively with and become involved in meaningful and relevant ways in their children's early experiences in pre-schools, toddler groups and schools. At the same time, you and other practitioners in the children's workforce are aware that you need to understand the children's home and family environment much better to be able to effectively nurture and support their learning, well-being and development. Much of the knowledge about the child which professionals require is held by the parents; hence you have to develop strong and trusting relationships with them to be able to access it.

Before exploring the relationship between you as the Early Years Professional and parents it will be helpful to clarify the term 'parent'. From the Guidance to the Standards for the Award of Early Years Professional Status (Children's Workforce Development Council [CWDC], 2008) you will be familiar with the definition of parents as including:

> *Mothers, fathers, legal guardians and the primary carers of looked-after children.*
>
> (CWDC, 2008, p78)

The Guidance continues to point out that there may also be other significant adults in a child's life, for example a grandparent, an aunt or the new partner of the child's mother. These adults may spend a lot of time with a child, develop loving and supportive relationships with him and are generally seen as being responsible for him. They may also be your main contact with the child's family and be able to tell you much about the child's home environment. In legal terms, however, this does not mean they have parental responsibility which is defined much more strictly:

> *If the parents of a child are married to each other or if they have jointly adopted a child, then they both have parental responsibility. This is not automatically the case for unmarried parents.*
>
> *According to current law, a mother always has parental responsibility for her child. A father, however, has this responsibility only if he is married to the mother or has acquired legal responsibility for his child through one of these three routes:*
>
> * *(after December 1 2003) by jointly registering the birth of the child with the mother;*
>
> * *by a parental responsibility agreement with the mother;*
>
> * *by a parental responsibility order, made by a court.*
>
> *Living with the mother, even for a long time, does not give a father parental responsibility and if the parents are not married, parental responsibility does not always pass to the natural father if the mother dies.*
>
> (www.direct.gov.uk/en/Parents/ParentsRights/DG_4002954, 2008)

This highlights the potential discrepancy between who may be seen as the parent of a child and who holds responsibility for the child. It also raises the question of whom you should work with and engage in the dialogue about the child's learning, development and well-being. There may not be a general and clear answer to this and each child and her family may lead you to a different arrangement. It is important to be aware, though, that only parents with parental responsibility can sign consent forms and need to agree to others collecting their children. You may agree with the parents that, for example, the grandmother will bring and collect the child and also join the parent volunteer rota in your pre-school. Although the grandmother is playing a major role in supporting her grandchild's learning and well-being, you will still have to find ways of engaging the parents in their child's play and learning.

For the purposes of this book and your practical work of engaging with parents it will be useful to employ a wider definition of the term 'parents' than the one arising from the understanding of parental responsibility. In addition to mothers, fathers, legal guardians and the primary carers of looked-after children, we will therefore also include other significant adults in a child's life in this term.

Parents and home environment: their influence on young children

The quote at the beginning of the chapter stresses how important parents and the home environment are to a child. Before looking at the research evidence supporting this statement, you may want to do your own small research project.

REFLECTIVE TASK

Think about your own core values and beliefs. What is really important to you in your life? What do you hold to be absolutely true? You will have many values and beliefs but choose just a few and then start tracing them back through the years. Did you hold these values when you first started working? Were they there when you were at school?

Table 1.1 Core values and beliefs

Core value/ belief	During my working life	As a young adult	As a teenager at school	As a young child at home

Also consider who influenced the shaping of your values: friends, teachers, brothers and sisters, parents and so on.

FEEDBACK

Your table is likely to show many ticks in the right hand-column: the values that define you today originated in your family and in your early childhood. Even as a teenager or young adult, your parents' views and opinions had an impact on your thinking, either in the sense that you assimilated their values and beliefs or that you felt it necessary to distance yourself from them. Many values and beliefs may be implicit in what you do without you being fully aware of them – these, too, are likely to have been formed during your very early years and they still fundamentally shape you as a person.

Your own experience is likely to tell you that most of your beliefs and values originated in the family you grew up in. This stresses the importance of the experiences in early childhood and of the influence parents have on children's lives. Research confirms that the home environment and parental involvement in learning activities have a substantial influence on a child's attainment in the Early Years and beyond. Siraj-Blatchford *et al* (2002) summarise that the involvement of parents in learning activities is closely linked to better cognitive attainment in the Early Years. In addition to supporting cognitive development, the quality of the learning environment in the home also has a strong influence on the social development of children (Daycare Trust, 2003). Desforges and Abouchaar (2003) whose research focussed on pupil achievement and attainment have found that parental involvement in children's learning in the home has a significant effect on children's achievements, in fact a greater effect than the quality of the schools. Apart from the correlation between higher parental involvement and higher attainment for the children, their research also highlights that parents get involved more when their children achieve more (see Figure 1.1 below).

Parents seem to be motivated by the success of their children and feel encouraged to continue and increase their involvement in their children's learning and development. In addition to this motivational influence, parental participation has a positive effect on how teachers perceive a child: it increases the teacher's expectations for the child (Einarsdottir and Gardarsdottir, 2009). This in turn encourages the child to do better and increases her academic achievements. The cycle in Figure 1.1 can therefore be extended to that in Figure 1.2.

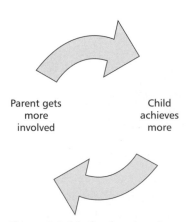

Figure 1.1 Motivational cycle with parent and child

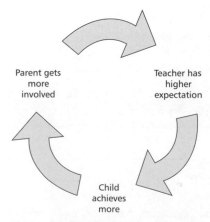

Figure 1.2 Motivational cycle with parent, teacher and child

This highlights how interrelated parent, child and Early Years practitioner are and how they influence each others' behaviour. It leads to the conclusion that Early Years Professionals have to work closely with parents as this enhances their work with children and improves the outcomes for children. Siraj-Blatchford *et al* (2002) expand further that where there is consensus and consistency between the learning at home and the curriculum at school, children achieve better outcomes. A joint approach from you and the parent will reinforce the learning in the one sphere with the same approach, expectations and strategies in the other, and children will not get different messages in their main care environments. How you can put partnership working with parents into practice will be explored further in Chapters 4, 5 and 6.

What parents gain from getting involved

The research evidence in the previous section shows how vital the involvement of the parent is in a child's learning and life. Most parents want to do the best for their children and are prepared to sacrifice their own interests, leisure time or convenience for this. Getting involved and being more active in their child's life and in the community they live in has positive effects for the parents as well. In the two case studies below you can see how two parents became involved – Sharon in community activities for families with young children and Louise in learning activities for parents in her children's nursery.

CASE STUDY

Sharon has been registered with Sure Start Cambridge since June 2004, after the birth of her second child. She was attending drop-ins regularly with a group of friends, but workers described her as shy and very quiet. While Julie, the parent forum worker . . ., was trying to develop the parent forum meetings she also spoke to Sharon but it wasn't until September 2005 that Sharon attended her first meeting. She soon became involved in organising and running the clothes swap . . . with a number of her friends and other parent forum members. This gave her more confidence and helped her to voice her opinions more. When the new chair and vice-chair for the parent forum needed electing, she was nominated and took on the role of chair. At this time she also started attending courses and groups without her friends. Throughout 2006 her involvement in Sure Start on behalf of the parents in Kings Hedges has gradually increased: she became parent board member in March 2006, opted to join the new steering group for the children's centre in Kings Hedges, attended shortlisting and interview sessions for crèche staff. Late in 2006 she was talking about her own development considering different training options and planning her return to work once her youngest child starts school.

(Sure Start Cambridge, 2007, p8)

Louise joined a Parents' Involvement in their Children's Learning (PICL) group at the Pen Green Centre when her eldest son was attending nursery. Louise comments, 'After learning about schemas and Leuven involvement I became a lot more tolerant . . . I began to understand why he was doing the things he was doing.' Louise and her family obviously gained enormously through Louise's greater understanding of her son's development (Tait, 2007, p50). Louise then started attending the PICL group again when her second child was at nursery and moved on to co-running a Growing Together group for parents with children under three.

Pre-schools have a long history of working with parents in their settings through parent rotas, parent committees, adult education courses and community activities. A study of adult learning in pre-schools undertaken by the National Institute of Adult Continuing Learning and the Pre-school Learning Alliance highlighted the benefits of parental involvement. Many parents reported making new friends and social contacts. Enabling parents to overcame feelings of isolation and helping them to develop support networks can limit poor mental health and feelings of depression. A further finding was that parents became more confident and reported increased self-esteem; many also developed the confidence to undertake learning opportunities and consider employment. Communication skills, social skills and practical skills (especially relating to work at committee level) all increased. A further significant finding was that parents who left school early and had few qualifications, first time parents, and parents with limited experience of employment made the greatest gains through involvement at pre-school (McGivney, 1998). These findings show clearly that parents benefit greatly from their involvement as far as their own development is concerned.

Children also gained from their parents' involvement in their Early Years setting as parents felt more confident in their parenting role. Talking to other parents and seeing a group of children helped them to put their own and their child's experiences into perspective. In addition, 'Many parents reported that they had learned to organise, structure and manage children's play and had acquired an understanding of how children learn through play. As a result, they were able to stimulate their own children in more creative ways at home and a number reported improved relationships with them.'

(McGivney, 1998, p45)

So far you have read about research into how important parents and the home environment are for a child and what impact the involvement in children's learning and Early Years settings can have for parents and children. In addition, the relevance of the relationship between Early Years Professional and parent has been highlighted. The next step is to start translating this theoretical knowledge into practice in your setting. Much of this will be covered in later chapters but initially it is useful to consider the information you collect before a child starts in your setting. There are a range of approaches Early

Years settings use to get to know children and to help child and parent settle into new environments and routines.

- Home visits.

- Information packs explaining the setting and the people in it.

- Open days.

- Visits.

- Information evenings.

- And many others.

There is normally a mix of information giving (professional to parent) and data collection (from parent to professional).

PRACTICAL TASK

Whether you use open days, information packs or home visits, examine the material closely and categorise which parts are about giving information to parents and about receiving information from them. Is there a good balance? Do both parents and professionals get the information they need? Ask some of the parents in your nursery whether they felt they had all the information they needed to make their child's start comfortable and easy. Ask your staff team whether they had enough information about the family to help the child settle in quickly.

FEEDBACK

Adults often find it easier to talk about the child rather than themselves, and professionals may feel uncomfortable with asking parents more personal questions about approaches to parenting and children. However, staff in Early Years settings benefit greatly from knowing more about the parent and the relationship between parent and child when planning good quality care and education for a child. You may want to extend the information you gather when a child first starts at your setting to include more details regarding the parents (resident and non-resident, if possible).

C H A P T E R   S U M M A R Y

In this chapter you explored the term 'parent' and established a working definition for this book: parents include mothers, fathers, legal guardians and the primary carers of looked-after children as well as other significant adults in a child's life who may not necessarily hold parental responsibility. You examined the enduring contribution parents make to their child's learning, development, and well-being and considered the interrelatedness of parent, child and teacher leading to the conclusion that Early Years Professionals have to work closely with parents to maximise outcomes for children. In addition to the positive impact on their children, parental involvement and participation also enhances parents' confidence, skills and self-esteem. In recognition of the relevance of parents you have reviewed the initial contact you have with families to improve the information you gather before a child starts in your setting.

Self-assessment question

1. What do children gain from their parents' involvement in their Early Years setting?

Moving on

This chapter has outlined the importance of the relationships between child, parent and professional and highlighted the need for strong partnership working. The relationships in this triangle will be further explored in Chapter 3 including how socio-economic factors and parental education influence involvement and children's learning. Different approaches to engaging parents in their child's learning and in your setting and to working in partnership with them will be examined in Chapters 4, 5 and 6. Chapter 5 will also explore in more detail how you can work with parents who do not regularly come into your setting.

REFERENCES

Children's Workforce Development Council (2008) *Guidance to the standards for the award of Early Years professional status.* Leeds: CWDC. (**www.cwdcouncil.org.uk**).

Daycare Trust (2003) Focus on effective provision of pre-school education. *Partners,* 27: 6–7.

Department for Education and Skills (2007) *Every parent matters.* Nottingham: DfES Publications. (**www.teachernet.gov.uk/everyparentmatters**).

Desforges, C and Abouchaar, A (2003) *The impact of parental involvement, parental support and family education on pupil achievements and adjustment: A Literature Review* (Research Report 443). Nottingham: DfES Publications.

Directgov – Public services all in one place (2008) *Parental Rights and Responsibilities.* (**www.direct.gov.uk/en/Parents/ParentsRights/DG_4002954**).

Einarsdottir, J and Gardarsdottir, B (2009) Parental Participation – Icelandic playschool teachers' views, in Papatheodorou, T and Moyles, J (eds), *Learning together in the early years – exploring relational pedagogy.* London: Routledge.

McGivney, V (1998) *Adult learning in pre-schools.* Leicester: National Institute of Adult Continuing Education and Pre-school Learning Alliance.

Siraj-Blatchford, I, Sylva, K, Muttock, S, Gilden, R, and Bell, D (2002) *Researching effective pedagogy in the Early Years* (Research Report RR356), Department of Educational Studies, University of Oxford. London: DfES.

Sure Start Cambridge (2007) *Parent involvement evaluation report.* (Unpublished document).

Tait, C (2008), Getting to Know the Families, in Whalley, M and the Pen Green Centre Team (ed) *Involving parents in their children's learning.* London: Paul Chapman Publishing.

FURTHER READING

Department for Eduation and Skills (2007), *Every Parent Matters.* Nottingham: DfES Publications, (**www.teachernet.gov.uk/everyparentmatters**).
This will give you a better understanding of the Government's approach to working with parents, the benefits it sees in it and the commitment it is making to support parents.

McGivney, V (1998), *Adult learning in pre-schools.* Leicester: National Institute of Adult Continuing Education and Pre-school Learning Alliance.
The summaries of the interviews with parents give a very good insight into how parents see their involvement in Early Years settings.

USEFUL WEBSITES

www.parentlineplusprofessionals.org.uk
Parentlineplus is a national charity working with and for parents. Their website for professionals offers help in your work to support families.

2 Parents and what we think about them

CHAPTER OBJECTIVES

After reading this chapter you should be able to:
- assess critically the roots of assumptions made about parents;
- analyse the validity of some stereotypical views of parents in an Early Years context;
- identify effective values for the partnership work with parents.

This chapter develops your knowledge and understanding of discrimination against parents and approaches to overcoming it. The content is particularly relevant to 'S3', 'S29', and 'S30', because these standards require you to reflect on your relationships with parents and on your approach to working in partnership with them to enhance their children's learning. The chapter also links to 'S35' and 'S38' which address your reflection on and modification of practice in your setting. The learning from this chapter will develop your expertise in the area of effective communication and engagement as outlined in the Common Core of Skills and Knowledge for the Children's Workforce. You will look at a range of assumptions about parents, and stereotypes or prejudices about fathers and mothers regularly encountered in daily life. In particular the chapter will look at assumptions Early Years staff may make about parents. As you become more aware of these you will be able to reflect on how they influence your own practice and the work of others in your setting. The chapter will encourage you to consider values and beliefs that support partnership working with parents in your setting.

Our internal picture of parents

In Chapter 1 you explored the origin of your values and beliefs and concluded that many of them developed in childhood. This is supported by Rodd (2006) when she states that Early Years practitioners and parents alike develop their beliefs about children in their families of origin. Developing beliefs and values so very early in life often means that we see them as facts without considering whether they are true or not. You may be familiar with the Anti-Bias Curriculum developed in the USA. It gives practitioners a tool to work with children of pre-school and nursery age to address pre-prejudice and stereotypes. It stresses how early the foundations are laid for later prejudices (often before the age of three years) and the harm they can do to a child's development by narrowing his view of other people and his reluctance to engage with them (Derman-Sparks and the ABC Task Force, 1993). As an Early Years practitioner you recognise pre-prejudice and early stereotypes in the play and behaviour of young children and address them. However, you may not have the same level of awareness for stereotypes and beliefs which were formed in your own childhood and which are the basis for your current actions and behaviour.

REFLECTIVE TASK

Think back to your own childhood and reflect on what 'parents' mean to you. Did you grow up in a large family or just with one parent? What characteristics or qualities of your parents do you remember in particular? Were there family rituals you particularly enjoyed – outings, celebrations, routines?

Your early experiences will have shaped your concepts of parents and families. Some of these concepts you will be aware of, others will be more subconscious, not at the surface of your awareness, and both will be shaping how you think about the parents you work with now. Do you compare the parents you work with now to your internalised picture of 'parents'? What does that mean for the way you relate to the parents you work with?

FEEDBACK

*To be able to develop constructive relationships with parents in your setting it is important not to pre-judge them but have an open mind to their way of life and their style of parenting. The Early Years Foundation Stage encourages practitioners to think of every child as a unique individual and to plan for his specific needs (Early Years Foundation Stage Effective Practice, **www.standards.dfes.gov.uk/eyfs/site/1/1.htm,** downloaded 2008). The same principles should be applied to his parents and family – they are as unique as he is. Taking time to get to know individual parents, their interests, concerns and ideas will prevent you stereotyping them as well as ensuring that they feel more valued and respected. This in turn will lay the foundation for effective partnership working.*

External messages

In addition to the beliefs and values formed during your own childhood there are numerous other, either subtle or very explicit, messages influencing how you see families and parents – in papers and books, on television and on the radio. Adverts show mothers glowing with delight when their children step into the house covered in mud; fathers joyfully drive their children around; smiling grandparents take their grandchildren on outings.

PRACTICAL TASK

Choose a selection of children's books either from your setting or from the library and study how parents are portrayed in them, firstly, in the pictures and illustrations and secondly, in the text or story itself.

FEEDBACK

The images of mothers, fathers, and carers are rarely realistic in relation to ethnicity, disability and other factors, and often reflect common stereotypes regarding gender roles and traditional family make-up. A recent study by Seden (2008) showed, among other things, that parents do not necessarily identify with the way in which they are portrayed in children's books. Parents also commented that in many books children were shown to play on their own rather than with a parent (either playing with them or being nearby). This gives subtle messages to parents and children – but not necessarily the message Early Years Professionals would like to give parents about the importance of them getting involved in their children's play and learning.

In the media many groups of parents are stereotyped, for example single parents, teenage mothers, stepfathers, and parents of large families. There is no scope here to explore all of these but it is useful to consider at least one group as an example. Teenage parents are often accused of becoming pregnant to receive state welfare benefits or to be moved to better housing; they are seen are promiscuous and irresponsible; there is an assumption that they are bad parents. As established earlier, each child and each parent is unique and you should strive in your setting to meet their individual needs. The best people to tell you about their needs are the parents themselves. Through a mix of interviews, surveys and brainstorming events young parents in Newham were encouraged to express what was important to them so that professionals could provide better services for them. Here is a selection of the views.

Young parents said they wanted not to be judged:

- to beat the social prejudices about them being irresponsible parents;

- and have projects that embrace the good side of being young parents not just hard times;

- to be treated respectfully by health professionals, midwifes and social workers.

Young parents said they wanted to learn how their children develop:

- more than just behaviour management, young parents wanted to learn how to help their children learn and grow;

- to feel reassured that they are doing the best for their children;

- to know that their children are learning while they are.

Community Links, www.community-links.org/images/uploads/YoungParents.pdf,
24 September 2008, pp2–3.

In this project young parents expressed a strong desire to support their children's well-being, development and learning, just like other parents would, and accusations that they may be bad parents or irresponsible are difficult to justify in the face of their comments. At the same time there are clear messages that professionals are not always as supportive as young parents would like or need them to be. Assumptions and prejudices may act as barriers to effective communication and hinder good working relationships with teenage parents.

How do you work with teenage parents in your setting? Are you providing an environment they feel comfortable in?

Children's centres are specifically charged with supporting young parents and are likely to work with several at any one time; in small rural pre-schools there may not be any teenage parents for months. Your services for teenage parents will therefore vary greatly. It is important, though, to be aware of their particular needs and offer a welcoming and supportive environment for them. You may want to ensure that your local Connexions office is aware of your services so that they can signpost young pregnant women and teenage parents to you. Your local Connexions office will also be a good source of information for you on what services teenage parents may want, or how you can make your setting more welcoming to them. In addition to Connexions there may be voluntary sector organisations in your area working with teenage parents. Their expertise could be invaluable to you. (If you want to check where you nearest Connexions office is, go to www.connexions-direct.com.)

Professionals' views of parents

The relationship between Early Years Professional and parent is a special one, as parents entrust the care for their dearest and most vulnerable relative, their child, to you. The expectation is that staff members in Early Years settings focus their energies on supporting the children in their development, learning and well-being. However, this can not be done in isolation from the parents and, like the wider population, Early Years practitioners have personal views of parents, which have an impact on the way they perceive and interact with them. In any situation it would be very hard to build trusting and supportive relationships if one partner held negative or misplaced views of the other. In the interest of children it is particularly important that teachers approach parents with positive attitudes as there is a correlation between teachers' views of parents and parents' views of the school or pre-school. Knopf and Swick (2007) found that when teachers see parents more positively, parents feel better about the care and teaching in their school or pre-school. As a consequence, the levels of parents' involvement in their children's learning in the Early Years setting increases (also see Figure 1.2 on page 4). Exploring and addressing the stereotypes found amongst teachers is therefore essential to create the right environment and ethos in which positive relationships can flourish. Knopf and Swick (2007) found that some teachers thought that parents did not care, that they did not have the time or motivation to get involved, and that they were not interested in leadership roles. We will explore these three assumptions in more detail but you may well encounter others in your Early Years setting.

Stereotype: parents do not care

If parents do not participate in activities in the Early Years setting teachers are more likely to conclude that they do not care about their child (Lawrence-Lightfoot, 2003, in Knopf and Swick, 2007). However, parents can express their care, interest and love in different ways, just as they prefer different ways of getting involved in their child's Early Years experiences. In addition to personal preferences, external factors may also prevent them from participating, for example their shift pattern or the need to care for an elderly relative. The Pre-school Learning Alliance estimates that 140,000 parents are involved in supporting the running of voluntary or private Early Years settings. Private and voluntary organisations account for only 40 per cent of the whole Early Years sector and thousands of parents participate in nursery schools and classes (Penlington, 2002). The total number of parents involved in activities in Early Years settings is therefore considerably higher. Every year approximately 84 per cent of the families using the Pen Green Centre take part in activities in the classroom, workshops, research projects and, most importantly, in activities that support their children's learning in the Centre and at home (Tait, 2008). This shows that parents care and are keen to get involved. However, conditions and circumstances may not always be supportive and settings have to explore with parents how they can best facilitate participation.

CASE STUDY

Leanne had been coming to the messy play sessions of the Sure Start Local Programme with her son for a few weeks. She was keen for him to be with other children and did not mind him trying out the new and messy activities. She normally remained standing, keeping well away from the actual activities, sometimes chatting to other parents but rarely sitting down with Callum to help him to explore the new and exciting materials. This was noted by Bobby, the group leader, who began to observe mother and son more closely to see why Leanne would not get involved in Callum's play. During one session Callum was particularly enjoying the cornflour and water mixture. To start the discussion about the benefits of her involvement in Callum's play Bobby took the activity card from the table with her and joined Leanne a little distance away. After chatting a little while Bobby explained the cornflour activity to Leanne and showed her the card. Leanne commented that she had seen other parents use the activity cards – while their children were playing they would look at them and then encourage the child to try new or different ways of exploring and playing. Leanne admitted that she would love to do that with Callum as well but couldn't – she had tried during her first few visits to the sessions but became very embarrassed because she could not read very well. It took her such a long time to comprehend what the cards were saying that Callum normally drifted off to other activities before she could start joining him in his play.

It is not easy to describe what is meant by a 'parent who cares'. Leanne certainly cared for Callum and wanted him to play and learn. That is why she came back to the session in spite of her own embarrassment about her limited literacy skills. Parents have their own needs and sometimes require additional help to engage with their child or the Early Years setting. Early Years Professionals have to find ways of offering activities, information and support so that parents of all abilities can access them. In this case activity cards with pictures and fewer words may help; or Bobby could discuss one or two activity cards with Leanne every time she comes so that she can build up her knowledge of the benefits of play over a period of time; or it may be possible to find a volunteer 'buddy' for Leanne who could read cards out to her throughout the sessions.

Stereotype: parents do not have the time or the motivation to get involved

Leanne's example shows the motivation many parents bring with them when they attend, for example, a play session and their desire for their children to do well but they are not always aware of how they can help them. How you can facilitate parents' involvement in their children's learning will be explored in more detail in later chapters. For many parents time is an issue, especially when they are in employment or have other children or relatives to care for. It is often not a complete lack of time, though, that stops parents from participating in nursery activities but the fact that these activities take place at times that are not convenient to them. Early Years settings have to explore carefully the timing of events and potentially the need to run one activity at different times to make it accessible to a larger number of families. As the statistics quoted above demonstrate, parents are motivated to participate and will make time for it if conditions are right.

Stereotype: parents are not interested in leadership roles

The Planning and Performance Management Guidance for Sure Start Children's Centres recommends that parents are involved in all levels of decision-making in a centre and suggest that a parent forum may be a useful vehicle to help parents voice their views (Department of Education and Skills, 2006). Some children's centres have very active parent representation – as volunteers in group sessions, in the parent forum and at partnership board level. This demonstrates parents' interest in the services offered to their children and families and shows that they are willing to get involved in shaping, evaluating and promoting them. If there is honest interest in their views and the real possibility to contribute to the decisions within a setting, many parents are willing and able to take on leadership roles. This will be explored further in Chapter 4 where you will look at partnership working in management and leadership.

You can see from these three examples that some of the assumptions teachers and Early Years practitioners make about parents are unfounded. Some practitioners may argue that their own experience shows these assumptions to be true, in which case an exploration of how they have tried to engage with parents and encourage them to get involved may be useful. In later chapters you will consider an approach to parental involvement in your Early Years setting and in children's learning which is based primarily on the parents' interests, needs and circumstances rather than those of the setting.

A view of parents that supports partnership working

In Chapter 1 you considered the important role parents play in the lives of their children and drew the conclusion that professionals and parents have to work closely together to maximise outcomes for children. However, this working relationship may be clouded by prejudices and stereotypes. In this chapter you have examined internal pictures and external messages about parents in our daily lives, and you explored your own and other professionals' attitudes in relation to parents. Once aware of your own assumptions and prejudices you can evaluate how these influence your practice and your current relationships with parents. You may now also be in a better position to recognise the assumptions colleagues make about parents and stimulate the discussion in your staff team about how these could be overcome. For a team to work effectively together it is fundamental to share the same basic values and beliefs and not to let personal views and individual prejudices result in mixed messages to parents and children. Rather than tackling individual counterproductive assumptions you may want to take a more positive approach and explore your setting's overall ethos with regards to parents and agree together with your team what your underlying principles are and how these are expressed in your practice.

REFLECTIVE TASK

Consider what the values and beliefs are on which your setting bases or should base its work with parents.

FEEDBACK

Rodd (2006) summarises the values and beliefs she regards as fundamental for the development of partnership working with parents and you may find these are a good starting point for the work with your team.

Parents are:

- *experts on their children;*
- *significant and effective teachers of their own children;*

- *skilled in ways that complement those of practitioners;*

- *different but have equal strengths and equivalent expertise;*

- *able to make informed observations and impart vital information to practitioners;*

- *inherently involved in the lives and well-being of their children;*

- *able to contribute to and central in decision-making;*

- *responsible and share accountability with practitioners.*

(Rodd 2006, p226)

You will already have processes and procedures in place in your Early Years setting to agree values and principles, but further suggestions of how you can work with your staff team to negotiate shared beliefs and ensuing practice can be found in other publications in this series.

C H A P T E R   S U M M A R Y

In this chapter you have looked at some stereotypes, prejudices and perceptions in relation to parents. They have different origins but parents' comments and experiences have shown how little justified these perceptions can be. Considering some stereotypes in more detail has led to the conclusion that there can be a misunderstanding between professionals and parents about parents' motivation to get engaged, about suitable practical arrangements and about levels of interest. Through reflecting on this you have had the opportunity to change your perception of parents which will provide you with a basis for the development of respectful and trusting relationships with them. A set of values for partnership working with parents has been suggested and you have started considering their implications for your own practice and for the work of your team.

Self-assessment question

1 Explain the importance of jointly held values and beliefs regarding the work with parents in an Early Years setting.

Moving on

This chapter has focussed on how we see parents and what we think about them. The next chapter is going to explore the relationships between parents and Early Years Professionals and develop the concept of partnership working. Chapter 4 will turn to the question of how we define 'involvement', what partnership means, and how and where parents can get involved in their child's learning and in the life of the Early Years setting. Chapters 4 and 5 will also give you an opportunity to see the values discussed here applied in a range of different settings and contexts.

Community Links, *What young parents really want – innovative ideas for service providers.* (**www.community-links.org/images/uploads/YoungParents.pdf,** downloaded on 24 September 2008).

Department for Education and Skills (2006) Sure start children's centres planning and performance management guidance. (**www.surestart.gov.uk**, downloaded on 15 January 2008).

Derman-Sparks, L and the ABC Task Force (1993) *Anti-bias curriculum – tools for empowering young children.* Washington: National Association for the Education of Young children, 7th printing.

Early Years Foundation Stage. (downloaded from **www.standards.dfes.gov.uk/eyfs/site/1/1.htm** on 24 September 2008.)

Knopf, H and Swick, K (2007) How parents feel about their child's teacher/school: implications for early childhood professionals. *Early Childhood Education Journal,* 34(4): 291–296.

Lawrence-Lightfoot (2003), in Knopf, H and Swick, K (2007) How parents feel about their child's teacher/school: implications for early childhood professionals. *Early Childhood Education Journal,* 34(4): 291–296.

Penlington, G (2002) *The parental stake in pre-school education.* London: The Social Market Foundation and The Pre-school Learning Alliance.

Rodd, J (2006) *Leadership in early childhood.* Maidenhead: Open University Press.

Seden, J (2008) Creative connections: parenting capacity, reading with children and practitioner assessment and intervention. *Child and Family Social Work,* 13: 133–143.

Tait, C (2008) Getting to know the families, in Whalley, M and the Pen Green Centre Team (ed) *Involving parents in their children's learning.* London: Paul Chapman Publishing.

Knopf, H and Swick, K (2007) How parents feel about their child's teacher/school: Implications for Early Childhood Professionals, *Early Childhood Education Journal,* 34(4): 291–296.
This brief article explores the interrelatedness of teachers and parents, misconceptions about parents, and practical ideas on how to develop positive ways of working with parents.

Stacey, M (2009) *Teamwork and collaboration in Early Years settings.* Exeter: Learning Matters Ltd.
This book explores how staff members work together and what impact their collaboration and team-working has on the services they offer for children and their families.

USEFUL WEBSITES

www.savethechildren.org.uk/en/5311_6733.htm
Offers a valuable range of resources and publications regarding anti-discriminatory practice.

www.equalityhumanrights.com
General information on human rights, diversity and equality issues.

3 The child–parent–EYP triangle

CHAPTER OBJECTIVES

After reading this chapter you should be able to:
- assess critically the relevance of the child and parent relationship for the Early Years Professional;
- analyse the role of the Early Years Professional in the parent and professional relationship;
- assess the influence of the parent and professional relationship on the well-being, development and learning of children.

This chapter develops your knowledge and understanding of relationships between Early Years practitioners, parents and children. The content is particularly relevant to 'S29', 'S30', and 'S31', because these standards require you to reflect on your relationships with parents and on your approach to working in partnership with them to enhance their children's learning. The chapter links to 'S2', 'S3', S7', 'S23' and 'S25' as it explores your understanding of individual children's development and the relationships you form with them. The application of the knowledge and understanding gained in this chapter will support you to develop trusting and effective relationships with parents and children and will increase your expertise in the area of child development as outlined in the Common Core of Skills and Knowledge for the Children's Workforce (DfES, 2005).

Introduction

Children normally develop their first relationships with their parents. These are crucial as they are the secure base for children's emotional and social development and act as models for later relationships. When children come into Early Years settings they develop new relationships with their key worker and other professionals but these are shaped by the children's earlier experiences. Both parent and Early Years practitioner are very significant elements in a child's life which affect not just his childhood development but also his well-being in later years. It follows therefore that parent and professional should work closely together, agree learning priorities for the child, and set the same expectations and boundaries in the home and in the Early Years setting. However, the relationships with the parents are often not in the forefront of Early Years Professionals' considerations when caring for the child.

In this chapter you will analyse this relationship between Early Years Professional and parent from two angles. Firstly, you will look at what parents expect from their partnership

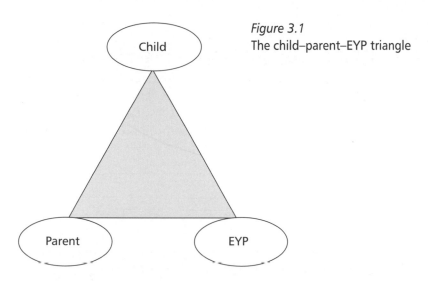

Figure 3.1
The child–parent–EYP triangle

with Early Years Professionals and at how parents' willingness to engage in this relationship can be increased. Secondly, you will examine which factors support the engagement of Early Years practitioners in the partnership with parents with a specific emphasis on your leadership role regarding staff development and training. However, as a child's first relationship is the one with the parent the chapter will start with a brief look at the diverse family and community contexts in which parents bring up their children. The focus will then move to the attachment between parent and child reflecting on the relevance of this relationship for your own work and considering how you can support attachment and parenting in the context of an Early Years setting. The relationships between yourself and the children will form the majority of your studies for Early Years Professional Status and will therefore not be explored in great detail here apart from those factors in this relationship which have a bearing on the co-operation between professionals and parents.

Child and parent

One child and one parent are already a family but families can bring together a varying number of people of different ages and generations, related or not related, in the same household or living apart. Chapter 1 mentioned the issues surrounding parental responsibility and how this does not necessarily rest with the natural father, or with the adults living in the same household as the child. You may regularly work with children growing up in step-families, or children who are being brought up by their fathers alone. Some children are looked after by foster parents or live in large families made up of three generations in the same household. There can be a considerable range of family set-ups amongst the group of children you work with in your setting just based on ages and biological relatedness. In addition, a family may also comprise two (or more) different religions or ethnic groups. In your work with children you have to be aware of the range of backgrounds and adjust your approach to the child in the classroom or nursery to accommodate and reflect her culture and family life style.

PRACTICAL TASK

*Try to find out more about the community the families in your setting live in. Your local City or District Council may be able to help or the Office for National Statistics which has a range of data on economic measures, household make-up, lifestyles, number of dependent children in different households etc. You can also find information on different educational indices and levels of qualifications on their website (**www.statistics.gov.uk**).*

FEEDBACK

Being aware of the wider community will enhance your understanding of the daily lives experienced by the children and parents in your setting and the issues or concerns some families face. On the basis of this understanding you may have to modify and adapt your approach to parents in order to establish fair and respectful relationships with them, for example by not expecting every family to contribute to the costs of an outing or, in neighbourhoods where literacy levels are low, by discussing sensitively with a parent how staff may help him to read and add comments in the home-school diary. Apart from gaining insights into family contexts, a detailed picture of the community will also provide you with an indication of the environment in which the relationship between parent and child develops. Whether their family set-up is common or not in the area can make a difference to how parents perceive themselves or to how isolated or supported they feel.

You may have discovered a discrepancy between the make-up of the community surrounding your setting and the families using it which may suggest the need to explore why some sections of the community are not accessing your setting. This question will be further examined in Chapter 5.

The parent and child relationship and the resulting attachment of the child to the parent are critical for the later development of the child as this attachment provides the basis for the child's emotional and social well-being and influences academic competence (Bowlby, 1969; Pianta, 1997). Pianta highlights the connection between the parent–child relationship and emotional development, self-regulation, attention and motivation, problem-solving, and self-esteem. If the child is securely attached to her primary caregiver or parent she is likely to achieve better outcomes at school. Supporting the attachment between parent and child is therefore an important task for all professionals working with families.

Fatema runs a weekly stay and play session in her community centre. The group is not large but about eight families attend regularly. Jane has brought her daughter Chloe (two years three months) for the last few sessions together with her four-month-old baby Ben. Chloe enjoys the different play activities on offer to the children and is keen to involve Fatema in them. When Fatema talks to Jane about Chloe's enthusiasm and praises her concentration and perseverance, Jane is not paying much attention. During the first half hour of several sessions Fatema has observed Chloe trying to get her mother to join in with her but Jane never does and Chloe spends the remaining time during the sessions playing either by herself, seeking Fatema's company or joining other family groups. Initially Fatema thought that Jane found it difficult to get involved in Chloe's play because she had to care for Ben but then started noticing that Ben was often left unattended in his baby seat while Jane was either talking to other parents or leaving the room to smoke outside.

On the grounds of her observations Fatema was concerned about Jane's interactions with her children which seem to lack consideration, warmth and understanding of the children's needs. She arranged for a volunteer to help with the running of the sessions and started spending more time with Jane modelling how she can help Chloe to enjoy the play activities and how to talk to and play with Ben.

Fatema saw that the relationships between Jane and Chloe, and Jane and Ben were not developing towards a secure parent–child attachment which would support the learning and well-being of the children. She can address this in the context of her stay and play sessions but may find that additional help is needed. In many nursery schools and children's centres there is a strong emphasis on supporting the parent in her role either through play sessions providing an understanding of learning through play, through family drop-ins where parents can get advice and information on a range of different problems or through parenting courses. Many children's centres also work with midwives, health visitors, specialist nurses and child psychologists to help individual families improve the emotional and mental well-being of child and parent.

As mentioned above, a secure attachment between child and parent enhances a child's well-being and development in early childhood but also has benefits for later years. However, the development of this attachment does not stand alone but is linked to good parenting skills in general. In their evaluation of the parenting support available in Sure Start Local Programmes Barlow, Kirkpatrick and Stewart-Brown (2008) demonstrate the correlation between the short-term outcomes associated with good parenting and the longer-term outcomes for children and young people as shown in Table 3.1.

The correlation between the short-term outcomes associated with good ...nd the longer-term outcomes for children and young people

...ing and parenting support in ... Early Years lead to	In the long-term, children will have
Secure attachment between parent and child	Fewer behaviour problems
Self-esteem	Achieve better outcomes at school
Emotional regulation	Less likely to become delinquents
Capacity to communicate	Fewer mental health problems
Capacity for relationships	Less likely to smoke or use drugs
	Reduced sexual promiscuity

Adapted from Barlow, Kirkpatrick and Stewart-Brown (2008)

As mentioned above, Early Years settings can support parents in many different ways to enhance their children's attachment and their own parenting skills in general through informal drop-ins, parenting courses or specialised home-visiting schemes. In smaller settings without professionals from other disciplines, it is important that staff members develop a good knowledge of other organisations and groups in the area so that parents can be made aware of parenting support available to them from other sources.

REFLECTIVE TASK

Assess your current practice – how are you supporting the development of the parent–child relationship? Can parents easily access further support and advice when they need it?

FEEDBACK

An important element in supporting parents to develop strong relationships with their children is the understanding of the relevance of attachment, which factors contribute to it and what impact it has on a child's life. You may therefore want to share your knowledge with parents in informal chats, by making written information available or in structured workshops and courses. Furthermore, you can support the development of secure attachments by creating opportunities for parent and child to enjoy interacting with each other, for example during a baby massage session, and for parents to meet, make friends and develop supportive social networks.

Child and Early Years Professional

As mentioned above the relationship between child and professional form the major part of the Early Years Professional Standards and you will explore all aspects of it elsewhere as you prepare for your assessments. In this book it is therefore sufficient to draw attention to the aspects which involve the child directly in the work of the Early Years Professional with the parent. Further to your considerations of attachment and parenting support it is worth noting that there is an additional aspect to the attachment between parent and child, which is its impact on Early Years practitioners. The early relationship between parent and child forms the model for later relationships which include the child's relationship with her carer at pre-school or teacher at nursery. Like the child and parent relationship this can be close and affectionate, distant and formal, or characterised by conflict (Pianta, 1997). Furthermore, it influences the child's adjustment to the Early Years setting (adjustment referring to the levels of motivation, attention, self-esteem, communication, problem-solving ability and peer-relationships) and can predict the success or failure at later stages of schooling depending on its quality. Pianta (1997) has explored teachers' reports on their attachment relationships with individual children and found that when teachers report children to be more securely attached to them, they also report higher levels of competence in the classroom. If children change from one teacher to another, there is a correlation between the changes in attachment and their adjustment in the classroom, for example if the relationship moves towards conflict, adjustment drops; if attachment becomes closer, adjustment rises (Pianta, 1997). For staff in Early Years settings this highlights the relevance of stable key working arrangements which allow children to develop close and trusting relationships with one staff member. It also stresses the need for Early Years Professionals to pay close attention to the relationship between parent and child. If this relationship is not nurturing, loving and supportive, then the child may find it difficult to build good relationships with key workers in nurseries or pre-schools. This adds to the argument that supporting parents is a relevant and essential task for Early Years practitioners.

Parent and Early Years Professional

Before we explore your relationship with the parent in the triangle of parent, child and professional, it is helpful to consider the Early Years Professional herself/himself. There are many skilled and experienced professionals working towards achieving Early Years Professional Status, but your professional development journeys will vary greatly. Some work in pre-schools, others in reception classes or in day nurseries, and others are childminders working in their own homes. There will be some who work in teams, while others are supported by networks or less formal support groups. The teams can be very small, for example in a small rural pre-school, while others may be very large and consist of professionals from several different disciplines, for example in a large children's centre. Some of the staff you lead will be highly skilled and experienced, others may be at the start of their careers, and some Early Years Professionals may lead a mixed team of staff and volunteers. This considerable variety means that you are all working in very different environments and will be approaching your work and partnerships with parents in quite different ways. This also means that there is not going to be one method that will be right for everybody but different approaches will work for different professionals and in different circumstances.

The variety also extends to the families, children and parents you meet in your setting. At the beginning of this chapter we have already mentioned the range of lifestyles families choose and the diverse circumstances in which children grow up. Parents in particular come from different backgrounds and have very different life experiences. Some may have had very poor experiences at school, some may have grown up in difficult economic situations; some may have had very supportive parents whom they can look to as role models, others may not have been well cared for in their childhoods. These life experiences shape parents and the way in which they engage with you. At the same time your own experiences and professional circumstances will influence your response to particular situations and individual parents. It will take time and perseverance to find the right approach which will help individual parents and professionals to communicate effectively with each other and even in an established relationship the dynamics can change unexpectedly. This demands of the professional a high level of flexibility and sensitivity and excellent communication skills. In addition, there needs to be an understanding that the work with parents is never static but forever changing and developing and, because of the large number of different backgrounds, needs, and experiences coming together, Early Years settings have to utilise a range of different methods and approaches to engage all parents.

Parents' own backgrounds and experiences have an impact on how they engage with their children's Early Years experiences and later schooling. Desforges and Abouchaar (2003) have carried out a literature review exploring, among other issues, the impact of parental involvement on pupil achievements and attainment and have identified some factors which influence this engagement. Although much of the research was based on parents of school-aged pupils rather than pre-school-aged children, there are valuable conclusions for all professionals wanting to work with parents. Better educated mothers are more likely to get involved in their children's Early Years settings, as are mothers from higher social classes. If parents face material deprivation or they are single parents, they are less likely to get involved in school activities. If a mother suffers with poor mental health and is socially isolated, she is also less likely to take part in events and activities offered to her by Early Years settings or schools. The influence of ethnicity on parental involvement and pupil achievement is more complex as ethnicity and socio-economic status are closely linked. However, ethnicity itself has only a very small influence, and parental aspirations and expectations are much more important in relation to pupils' achievements (Desforges and Abouchaar, 2003).

It is important to stress that the majority of parents are keen and interested in getting involved in their children's learning and schooling; however, some parents may find it more difficult than others and need additional help and support. Offering this support is particularly relevant in the light of the earlier discussion in Chapter 1 about how parents' involvement shapes the teacher's perception of the child, which in turn influences the child's achievements. Rather than drawing unfavourable conclusions for the child when parents do not engage with Early Years practitioners, questions should be asked why parents do not get involved and how they can be supported to participate.

In Chapter 2 you considered how Early Years Professionals and other staff members may perceive parents. In the context of the relationship between Early Years Professional and parent the reverse is also of interest; that is, the way parents view professionals and how they would like to be treated by them.

- *Parents want someone who cares about them and their children.*

- *Parents want respect and to be seen as an effective member of the child's education team.*

- *Parents want to have a part in shaping the agenda that impacts them.*

- *They want to see their ideas respected and used in creating quality care environments.*

- *Parents want competent early childhood professionals who deliver the services effectively and in ways that truly meet their needs.*

- *Parents want to be a part of a relationship that is collaborative and communicative.*

- *They want a close relationship with early childhood professionals.*

(Swick, 2004c quoted in Knopf and Swick, 2007, p293)

Swick's findings stress the high expectations parents have of Early Years staff; they want practitioners to be caring and competent. At the same time parents emphasise that they want to be involved and seek the relationship and partnership with professionals.

REFLECTIVE TASK

Reflect on your own practice when talking to and working with the parents in your setting. Would you meet the expectations Swick outlines? Where do you think you could make changes in your own practice?

In addition to the expectations about their involvement in Early Years settings, parents are also clear about how they would like other services, for example parenting or family support, to be delivered:

> Parents liked services to be practical, professional and well organized. They disliked services that did not give practical help, whose staff were not understanding, that were badly organized, inconvenient and expensive to use and, more important, that did not pay attention to their needs as they saw them. Services needed to steer a fine course between being seen as supportive to parenting and being seen as interfering. Bad feelings about a service were not because people felt that it was 'not for people like us' but because they felt that they had not been listened to or had been made to feel like bad parents.
>
> (Quinton, 2004, p61)

These comments from parents in the context of parenting support indicate that staff members need high level communication skills. Good listening skills, the ability to communicate with others as equals, a supportive but not interfering approach, and the avoidance of subtle negative messages are all important. Staff members need to be able to adjust their communication skills quickly and diplomatically to a range of different partners and contexts.

You have already reflected on your own practice regarding working with parents but parents' high expectations relate to all staff members. In your role as leader of practice in your setting you will have to consider up to which extent team members meet these expectations. The Pen Green Centre in Corby has for many years worked very successfully with parents and children. They realised at an early stage that staff members who were less experienced in working with adults found it difficult to engage parents in children's learning and addressed this with extensive and supportive staff training and development schedules (Tait, 2008). Rodd (2006) agrees and sees the lack of training in working in partnership with parents as a factor contributing to the anxiety and frustration many Early Years practitioners experience when engaging with parents. However, she goes a step further and suggests that staff members at the beginning of their career lack the necessary maturity to empathise and effectively engage with parents.

> *A shift in maturity, as well as a broader perspective, is considered to be the stimulus for identification with parents and families as well as children. At earlier stages of career development and professional maturity, relationships with parents are more likely to be authoritarian and paternalistic, token in nature and from a deficit perspective – that is, where parents, even those who are considerably older than the staff member, are not thought to possess the knowledge and skills necessary for bringing up their children. This approach is unlikely to empower parents to develop skill and competence in their own lives.*

> (Rodd, 2006, p230)

PRACTICAL TASK

Carry out a small audit summarising your team's training and experience in relation to working with adults and parents. In addition, reflect on their levels of maturity and stages of career development.

FEEDBACK

The information you have gathered should provide you with a good baseline for a staff development plan focussed on parental involvement work. You will have a system in place for addressing identified training needs within your setting either through training days for the whole team, courses for individual staff members, or more informally in small groups, through mentoring or supervisions. Whichever method you prefer, the National Occupational Standards for Work with Parents may be a useful tool to help you in your work with team members. The framework for the Standards will be familiar to you from your work towards the Early Years Professional Status: the Standards consist of principles and values for the work with parents, list detailed standards for different aspects of this work, outline performance criteria and summarise the required knowledge and under-standing. Not all of them will be relevant but the following may be helpful.

- *Contribute to building relationships in work with parents.*
- *Build and maintain relationships in work with parents.*
- *Communicate effectively with parents.*
- *Work with parents to meet their children's needs.*

(National Occupational Standards for Work with Parents, 2005).

There are also some Standards which support you to lead the work with parents in your setting, for example:

- *support others in developing their practice;*
- *provide services that meet parents' needs;*
- *provide leadership to your team.*

(National Occupational Standards for Work with Parents, 2005)

In exploring the relationship between parent and Early Years Professional we have considered what parents expect from the relationship and from the professionals looking after their children and in doing so the need for experience and training in the work with parents has emerged. Once staff members feel more confident and want to engage actively with parents it is essential that they have the time to do so. Building relationships takes time, it will not happen with one home visit and a brief chat when children are being dropped off in the morning. Giving staff members the time they need to talk and be available to parents should be planned into their daily routines and weekly rotas. In addition to contact time with children and non-contact time for planning, recording, and liaising with colleagues it seems beneficial to allocate staff members contact time with parents.

C H A P T E R   S U M M A R Y

In this chapter you have looked at the different relationships in the child, parent and Early Years Professional triangle. In the child-parent relationship early attachment is particularly important as it influences children's long-term well-being and their achievement at school. The relationship between child and Early Years practitioner builds on the earlier relationship and similarly correlates to children's adjustment at school. Because of this crucial importance of a child's relationship with her parent we concluded that Early Years settings should support the development of parenting skills and facilitate access to family support services.

The relationship between Early Years practitioner and parent is shaped by the life experiences and backgrounds of both partners and is therefore characterised by great variety. As a consequence professionals need to be very flexible in their approach to parents and use a range of different methods and strategies. You explored parents' expectations of Early Years practitioners and identified their wish to engage and work in partnership with professionals. To be able to meet these parental expectations it may be necessary to provide training opportunities for Early Years practitioners as their lack of experience in the work with adults often acts as a barrier to the successful engagement with parents. We identified the National Occupational Standard for Work with Parents as a potential tool to help you address the training needs in your team.

Self-assessment questions

1 Outline the importance of early attachment between child and parent.

2 In the light of parents' comments about how they would like services to be delivered, how should professionals relate to and communicate with parents?

Moving on

In this chapter we have introduced some factors influencing parental involvement. These will be explored in more detail in the next chapter together with the practical aspects of parental engagement and involvement in your setting and the strategies you can develop to enhance partnership working between professionals and parents. Barriers to involvement and approaches to engaging with parents who are not currently coming into your setting will be explored in Chapter 5. In Chapter 6 you will look at adult learning which will include ways in which you can support parents to enhance their parenting skills. Although the chapter will make reference to staff development, you may want to look to other books in this series for a more detailed consideration of how you can meet the training needs identified in your team.

REFERENCES

Barlow, J, Kirkpatrick, S, Steward-Brown, S (2008) Parenting support in Sure Start, in Anning, A and Ball, M (eds), *Improving services for young children, from Sure Start to children's centres,* London: SAGE Publications Ltd.

Bowlby, J (1969) *Attachment and loss: vol 1 attachment.* New York: Basic Books.

Desforges, C and Abouchaar, A (2003), *The impact of parental involvement, parental support and family education on pupil achievements and adjustment: a literature review.* (Research Report 443). Nottingham: DfES Publications.

Knopf, H and Swick, K (2007), How parents feel about their child's teacher/school: implications for early childhood professionals, *Early Childhood Education Journal,* 34(4): p291–296.

National Occupational Standards for Work with Parents (2005), (**www.parentinguk.org/2/standards,** downloaded on 9 October 2008).

Pianta, RC (1997) Adult–Child relationship processes and early schooling. *Early Education and Development*, 8(1): 377–388.

Quinton, D (2004) *Supporting parents: messages from research*. London and Philadelphia: Jessica Kingsley Publishers.

Rodd, J (2006) *Leadership in early childhood*. Maidenhead: Open University Press.

Tait, C (2008) Getting to know the families, in Whalley, M and the Pen Green Centre Team (eds) *Involving Parents in their Children's Learning.* London: Paul Chapman Publishing.

FURTHER READING

Barlow, J, Kirkpatrick, S, Steward-Brown, S (2008) Parenting support in Sure Start, in Anning, A and Ball, M (eds), *Improving services for young children, from Sure Start to children's centres.* London: SAGE Publications Ltd.
This article highlights factors linked to effective parenting support and interventions.

Desforges, C and Abouchaar, A (2003) *The impact of parental involvement, parental support and family education on pupil achievements and adjustment: a literature review.* (Research Report 443). Nottingham: DfES Publications.
The executive summary, Chapter 5 about ethnicity, parental involvement and pupil outcomes and Chapter 6 on differences between parents in the extent of their involvement are particularly interesting in the context of exploring why and how parents get involved. Other chapters will provide useful background reading for later parts of this study guide.

Whalley, M and the Pen Green Centre Team (2008) 2nd edition. *Involving parents in their children's learning.* London: Paul Chapman Publishing.
Whalley's descriptions of how staff at the Pen Green Centre work with children and their families offer examples of good practice which you may want to incorporate into your own work.

USEFUL WEBSITES

www.parentingacademy.org
This is the website of the National Academy of Parenting Practitioners.

www.natcen.ac.uk/natcen/pages/or_familiesandchildren.htm
Website for the National Centre for Social Research and its section offering research reports on Early Years and family issues.

4 Partnership working: involving parents in your setting

CHAPTER OBJECTIVES

After reading this chapter you should be able to:
- analyse the processes of initial engagement and ongoing involvement of parents in an Early Years setting;
- identify some features of effective communication with parents to enhance relationships;
- assess critically the opportunities for parental involvement and partnership working in your own setting;
- develop and implement strategies to enhance parental participation in all aspects of an Early Years setting, including children's learning.

This chapter develops your knowledge and understanding of parental involvement and partnership working between Early Years practitioners and parents. The content is particularly relevant to 'S3', 'S29', 'S30', 'S31', 'S32' and 'S35' because these standards require you to reflect on your relationships with parents and on your approach to working in partnership with them to enhance their children's learning. Through understanding the processes involved and the different strategies available you can enhance your own practice and influence the ethos and principles of your setting in relation to working in partnership with parents. The learning from this chapter extends the areas of effective communication, engagement and multi-agency working as detailed in the Common Core of Skills and Knowledge for the Children's Workforce (DfES, 2005).

Introduction

In this chapter you will look at working in partnership with parents at a practical level. Initially terms like 'involvement' and 'partnership' will be clarified leading to a discussion of the processes of involvement and partnership working. You will develop practical strategies to build relationships with the parents in your setting and to increase their involvement in the services you offer. You will examine how parents and staff members can work together to enhance children's learning in your setting and in their home environment before considering wider options for parents to make a contribution to their child's Early Years setting. While considering different areas of involvement you will have the opportunity to reflect on the role of the Early Years Professional in supporting and encouraging parents and practitioners to work in partnership.

Involvement and partnership

Before you can analyse the practical aspects of parental involvement and working in partnership with parents it will be necessary to gain a clear understanding of the concepts behind these terms, in the context of the Early Years sector. A look into the recent past will give an understanding of how the approach towards working with parents has changed. Before the 1960s Early Years and childcare workers saw themselves as experts as far as children were concerned and there was little co-operation between them and parents. In the 1960s society as a whole moved towards greater democracy and ordinary people became more involved in making decisions which affected their lives. In the Early Years sector it took some time for this approach to be accepted. Staff moved to an interventionist approach where working with families was based on the assumption that something was missing in the families which professionals had to supply. This did not recognise the contributions parents make to their children's lives and did not allow meaningful co-operation to develop between staff and parents. The 1970s brought a focus on communication; Early Years practitioners recognised that parents would think them more professional if they communicated more and developed positive relationships with them. This changed to a philosophy of accountability in the 1980s. Parents were seen as consumers of a service and Early Years settings began to work towards meeting their demands and wishes. At this stage parental involvement focussed on consultation and discussion of policies and procedures. In the 1990s the belief that parents had the right to control decisions that affected their children became embedded, leading to a demand for effective participation and active management by parents. The 1980s and 1990s also brought the recognition that parents were experts as far as their own children were concerned, leading to the Government expecting Early Years settings to work in true partnership with parents (Rodd, 2006, Arnold, 2008).

REFLECTIVE TASK

If you have many years' experience in the Early Years sector try to recall the development of your own values, beliefs and attitudes in relation to working with parents. Can you see similarities to the phases Rodd and Arnold identified? If you have started working in the Early Years more recently, consider where team members may be in the development of their values, beliefs and attitudes.

FEEDBACK

The Early Years sector has and still is undergoing a period of substantial change, with the shift in attitude to parental involvement representing just one aspect of it. In leading your team and aiming for more meaningful relationships with parents, individual staff members may need your support in reflecting on long-held views to find a way towards new ways of working without devaluing their past experiences and practices.

Rodd's comments on the relationships between Early Years practitioners and parents suggest a range of different understandings of the term 'involvement', while also using the terms 'engagement' or 'participation' synonymously (Rodd, 2006, Arnold, 2008). The Collins English Dictionary defines 'to involve' as: *to include or contain as a necessary part* (Collins English Dictionary 2001, p809). In some cases 'involvement' is specifically seen as 'involvement by parents in children's activities' (Siraj-Blatchford *et al*, 2002), while others have a much wider understanding:

> *Parental involvement takes many forms including good parenting in the home, the provision of a secure and stable environment, intellectual stimulation, parent–child discussion, good models of constructive social and educational values and high aspirations relating to personal fulfilment and good citizenship; contact with schools to share information; participation in school events; participation in the work of the school; and participation in school governance.*

> (Desforges and Abouchaar, 2003, p4)

In the light of these varied interpretations of the term 'involvement' it seems necessary to clarify what parents get involved in. This could be their children's learning in the widest sense, or classroom activities like reading with children, or management tasks as a member of the committee. It is also worth noting that teachers and parents may associate different contexts with the term. Teachers tend to think of involvement as a school-based activity which relates to children's learning or support in the classroom. Parents on the other hand view 'involvement' in much broader terms, often thinking about community-wide activities and engagement with and from groups outside the school itself (Knopf and Swick, 2007). For the purpose of our reflections in this book we will use the basic meaning of the term 'involvement' according to the Collins Dictionary, but clarify as much as possible the sphere in which the involvement or participation takes place.

Involving parents in your setting and in their children's early learning experiences is the first step which will, through the development of trusting relationships and over a period of time, lead to a partnership between parent and practitioner. The principles of an effective partnership in an Early Years setting are as follows.

- Both Early Years practitioners and parents are experts as far as children and families are concerned.

- Early Years practitioners and parents share responsibility for the children.

- It is a non-hierarchical, collaborative relationship.

- Both Early Years practitioners and parents make valuable though different contributions to the partnership.

(Rodd, 2006)

This leads to a concept of partnership working between parents and Early Years practitioners which is based a relationship of equals, in which both make valuable contributions and neither dominates the other. Both partners have an equal interest in the child's well-being, development and learning and decisions are made on the basis of negotiation. As you look more closely at where and how parents get involved in their children's learning in your setting, you will gain a deeper understanding of the characteristics of this partnership between yourself and parents in your particular context.

Getting started – accessing services

The first step to involving parents and working in partnership with them is encouraging them to use your service. This service could be the only service you offer, for example pre-school sessions, or part of a range of different services like a play session in a children's centre, or a parenting course in a nursery school. You can let parents know about your services by displaying posters, sending letters to all families, inviting partner organisations to signpost parents to your service and so on. However, encouraging parents to use your services and get involved in different activities is not a one-off event but a process including several steps as shown in Figure 4.1.

The initial contact can be made in a variety of ways, as described above. In addition, you or your setting may meet families in the local toddler group to tell them about your services; or parents get in touch with you because a neighbour has mentioned the music-and-movement sessions you offer. At this stage parents need help to understand what is on offer and to decide whether your service is right for them. Having received initial information families progress to visiting and then regularly using one of your services. For professionals the focus now shifts to encouraging comprehensive use of the service and helping families to develop contacts within the service, and to participate in individual activities. Supporting progression for the families is also part of this phase which will guide families to the next step, the use of additional services in a more independent way. Here the professional no longer needs to encourage the attendance at each session but remains available to give advice on further opportunities, support ongoing and more in-depth involvement, and progress learning and development for the family.

The nature and level of support which professionals offer in this process do not just vary with the different steps but also with the way in which parents generally access services. Some parents are very independent and autonomous in the way they approach and use services. Seeing a poster for a nursery outing is sufficient for them to put their name down and come along on the day. Other families need more encouragement to get involved; their access needs facilitating which may mean a staff member has to talk to the family on two or three occasions about, for example, a course you are planning to run. They need to be reminded beforehand and collected on the day. Others will set their own conditions for the use of services and only attend at times that suit them, or with staff members or

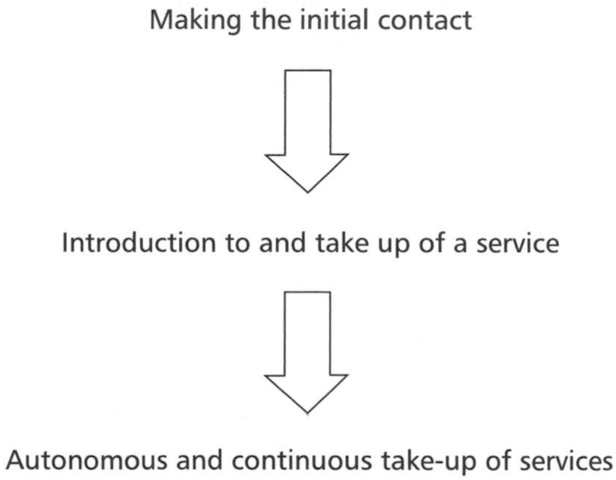

Making the initial contact

Introduction to and take up of a service

Autonomous and continuous take-up of services

Figure 4.1 Continuum of Access
Adapted from Garbers *et al*, 2006)

35

friends they feel comfortable with. For professionals the different approaches to service use mean that they have to gain a clear picture of what parents' preferences are and negotiate sensitively the arrangements which are acceptable to the family (for style of service use see Garbers *et al*, 2006).

CASE STUDY

Sam had already been in the pre-school for four months when his father Craig started to talk to staff about the problems he had recently with Sam's bedtime routine, which had turned into a tearful and stressful time. Sheila, the playgroup leader, felt that Craig would benefit from meeting some other fathers to share and discuss his problems and from some information on behaviour management to help him set new boundaries for Sam. Sheila recommended a fathers' group she had heard about in the primary school in the neighbouring village. As Craig was confident and sociable (he regularly volunteered during pre-school sessions and had joined the pre-school committee) she assumed he would make contact with the group himself. However, when she asked him about it a couple of weeks later, he had not been to the fathers' group meeting. With some careful questions, Sheila learnt that Craig felt quite uncomfortable with the idea of walking into a room of strangers and discussing the problems he was having with his son. They agreed that Sheila would get in touch with the group facilitator, Ben, and talk about Craig joining the group. She was able to arrange for Craig and Ben to meet during a pre-school session to get to know each other and shortly after that Craig joined the group meetings.

FEEDBACK

Craig felt comfortable with using one service (autonomous use), but he still needed support to access another, new service (facilitated use). Professionals should support parents depending on their levels of need especially when this level of need changes in the context of different problems or concerns. It is also important to realise that involvement is not a one-off event but a process; from getting involved in one service parents should be supported to get involved in another or in the same service in more advanced ways as this enhances their personal development. Normally confident service users may also need further support when new members join and the dynamics in the group change.

Building relationships

Once families access your services or setting you have to continue developing the relationship with them so that parents get involved in more activities or in detailed discussions about their children's learning, which can then lead to the development of your partnership with them. Much of this relationship will be defined by your values regarding parents and families and your attitude towards them (see previous chapters). A further factor in successful relationship building is the way in which you communicate

Figure 4.2 Developing relationships with parents

with parents. Figure 4.2 summarises some principles for the daily interactions with parents, which have been successful in the context of a Sure Start Local Programme.

The process of developing relationships with parents requires a considerable amount of time but once good relationships exist, partnership working can follow and you will find it easier to talk to parents about more sensitive issues; for example their child's aggressive behaviour during one of your sessions. It is important to be inclusive and non-discriminatory in your efforts to build relationships. Where there are language barriers, ways have to be found to overcome these so that the family is not excluded. You may have to employ different means of communication to ensure you cover the range of preferred communication styles. Some parents may prefer spoken information, while others respond better to written information, yet others may depend on pictures and other visual material.

How do you communicate with parents? Reflect on how parents may experience the chats or discussions you have with them and consider how you could interact with them more effectively.

Partnership working for children's learning

The findings of the research project Effective Provision of Pre-school Education stress that partnership working between Early Years settings and parents enhances children's lives.

The most effective settings shared child-related information between parents and staff, and parents were often involved in decision-making about their child's learning programme. This high level of parental involvement resulted in more intellectual gains for children. More particularly children did better where the centre shared its education aims with parents. This enabled parents to support children at home with strategies that complemented those being undertaken in the pre-school.

(Daycare Trust, 2003, p6)

The aim of your partnership work with parents in relation to children's learning is therefore to develop a joint approach with shared objectives, which both you and the parent can work towards in the setting and in the home respectively. As described above, for this partnership to work well, it is important to develop respectful and sensitive relationships with parents when they first come into your setting. Parents are particularly receptive to new learning when there are considerable changes in their lives, like the birth of a baby or the start at pre-school for an older child (see Chapter 6 for further details). There is therefore a window of opportunity for your Early Years setting; to explain to parents the way in which you could work with them; to enhance the learning and development of their child; to start the dialogue with them about what children learn in the setting and how the parent could support this learning at home with a view to establishing a partnership between parents and professionals for the benefit of their child.

Partnership working for learning in the setting

The context of your work with a parent in your sessions will vary depending on the nature of your setting. If you work in a children's centre a family may attend play sessions; in a nursery class the parent and child may visit together as part of the settling in process; in a pre-school parents may be volunteer helpers for the day. Regardless of the exact circumstance, your role will include role-modelling behaviour that supports children's learning, explaining the relevance of activities to parents and advising parents on a range of child and learning related questions. At the same time the parents will give you information about their child, his interests, and stage of development. Together you can discuss which activities in the setting may help to progress the child's learning.

CASE STUDY

Lisa has noticed that Magda is a little unsure about letting her daughter, Theresa, go to the easel and paint. Magda explains that Theresa is just painting her fingers and then smudges the paint all over the paper. Lisa opens up the discussion by asking whether Theresa has used paints before. It becomes clear that Theresa is more interested in exploring the texture of the paint than creating a picture. Lisa suggests that Magda and Theresa could try out some of the different messy play materials like shaving foam, wet sand and dry rice and compare them.

CASE STUDY *continued*

At the end of the session Lisa asks Magda how they have been getting on. Magda explains that she had not realised what messy play was all about but by walking round with her daughter and having a go herself, she could see how Theresa was discovering new textures. Some felt soft and smooth, others grainy and cold – they shared lots of new language. Lisa asks which material Theresa liked best and what Magda thinks she might like to explore next. They agree that next time it would be good to compare wet and dry sand, and look at different materials like felt, sandpaper and sponges. This would allow Magda to enforce some of the words learned in this session but also to introduce Theresa to new textures.

FEEDBACK

Lisa supported Magda to extend Theresa's learning during this session and through developing the dialogue with her they can now work together to support Theresa's development – Lisa by ensuring that relevant activities are available at the next session and Magda by enforcing the new words learned during this visit.

Parents will have very different levels of knowledge as far as child development is concerned and you have to observe and question them sensitively to establish where there may be gaps in their understanding. In general parents have a high awareness of the importance of their role in children's learning but feel they lack practical ideas about how to play with their child and what activities to offer them. In addition, they often neglect their children's cognitive and related language skills and do not encourage their thinking and problem-solving abilities sufficiently (Evangelou *et al*, 2008). You may therefore want to focus your partnership work with parents on the cognitive development of the children.

Parents may also come into your setting as parent-rota helpers or volunteers. In these roles they are not focussing on supporting their own child's learning but will engage with a small group or all the children in your setting. It may therefore be more appropriate to consider them as staff members rather than parents, and consequently give them detailed guidance on their role within the session or setting, invite them to access training opportunities which will develop their understanding of child development, learning and well-being, and offer them regular supervisory meetings.

PRACTICAL TASK

If you regularly work with parent helpers or volunteers, review what information you share with them on children's learning and development. Also consider how you gain feedback from them on the learning of the children they work with.

Giving the parent-rota helper a strong role in relation to the children's learning will enhance the importance of his role in the eyes of parents. If they feel their time in the setting has value for the children and is meaningful to them as well, then they are more likely to volunteer. If you request parents' help, but then only offer menial tasks, they will lose interest quickly.

Partnership working for learning in the home

Having explored how parents can participate in children's learning in an Early Years setting we now need to explore ways in which you and other Early Years practitioners can support and stimulate learning in the home environment. In the previous case study, Magda's increased awareness of her daughter's interests and learning is an important contribution to enhancing Theresa's home environment. Lisa could also give Magda some written information with suggestions on what to do at home, which new words she could introduce or which theories relate to the area of learning. Although this is valuable information material, it will only provide some brief general comments on a broad area of learning which may not help a parent to put their children's learning or behaviour into a wider development context. We have already acknowledged that parents would benefit from a deeper and more detailed understanding of children's cognitive development and learning. To help parents gain this and generally to support a better understanding of children's learning, development and well-being, it may be helpful to organise workshops or a course for them.

There are a large number of different courses available, some focussing on supporting learning, others address behaviour management, some are universal in their approach by addressing parenting in general, and others are very specific and explore just one aspect of development. Choosing one which suits your particular setting and your group of parents can be difficult, but the experience from the Sure Start Local Programmes highlights some factors of effective parenting support programmes which may be helpful. Although these are findings from interventions including other approaches to working with parents than courses, they are transferable.

> *What most of these interventions have in common, irrespective of the age of the child, is that they provide formalised ways to support parenting skills, often by providing additional skills, insight or understanding in terms of the parent's relationship with their child, and ways of parenting.*

> *In addition, these reviews suggest that:*

> - *manualised programmes with centrally-monitored, systemised delivery tend to deliver better outcomes;*
>
> - *programme integrity matters;*
>
> - *quality and training of staff is vital to programme success;*
>
> - *programmes that do not pay close attention to implementation factors are unlikely to be successful;*

- *successful programmes address more than one area of need, without losing sight of their core objectives;*

- *interventions that involve children as well as parents show better outcomes.*

(Barlow et al, 2008, pp139–140)

The Sure Start Local Programme experiences suggest that well-structured course materials and good monitoring features contribute to effective courses. Tutors or staff members delivering the course should be experienced and appropriately trained in adult education. The course approach should include work with the parent and the child, and go beyond the limitations of the course – that is, include an element of putting learning from the course into practice. This will increase the desired positive impact on the home environment with its considerable influence on the child's development and learning.

Providing the parent with information on children's learning and child development during a course or in a session will help the parent to gain insights into your work and the child's life in your setting, but is still mainly a one-way communication (especially if you are not the person delivering the course). Effective partnership work with parents requires two-way communication, parents not just receiving but also giving information. While you as an Early Years Professional will be able to provide the theory of child development, the parent is the expert regarding their child and his or her learning and development. These are both vital sets of knowledge which have to come together to plan effectively and achieve the best possible learning outcomes for the child.

There are many methods of sharing information which can form part of your partnership working with parents:

- parenting course focussing on child development;

- introductory workshop on children's learning;

- informal contacts during drop-off and collection;

- videoing at home and in the setting;

- joint training for staff and parents;

- handouts and information sheets;

- crèche feedback sheets;

- home-school diaries;

- frequent consultations;

- visits during sessions;

- discussion groups.

Each one of these methods on its own is simply a means of communication. It is the way in which they are utilised, combined, and embedded in an ethos of co-operation and trusting relationships between Early Years practitioners and parents which leads to effective partnership working.

Before a child starts at Butterfly Nursery she and her family visit for several sessions to get to know routines and staff members, and to become familiar with the Nursery's ethos and approach to learning. All parents are then invited to a series of workshops which focus on one aspect of child development at a time. During the consultation meeting the nursery teacher and the parent will decide which particular strands of learning are particularly relevant for the child and which activities in the home and in the setting can help to develop them. How the child engages with the activities and what she is learning will be shared and monitored by parents and professionals in the home-school diary until the next consultation when new activities or further areas of learning can be discussed.

Develop a plan for the processes you can use in your setting to enable staff members and parents to work in partnership and jointly agree learning activities and outcomes for children.

The exact shape of your plan will depend on the particular circumstances you work in. You may have to be flexible in your approach to be able to accommodate the most convenient arrangements for parents. They will not all respond well to the same methods and you will have to allow time to negotiate with individual families what works best for them. However, the core element of Early Years practitioners and parents working together to support and agree children's learning should always be included.

Partnership working to support the setting

Getting parents involved in their children's learning is essential but some parents may also want to get involved in your Early Years setting in others ways. For some parents an engagement outside the classroom and learning environment is a first step to building confidence and developing relationships with other parents and staff members. Offering a range of different opportunities to engage and participate is therefore important and gives parents a choice of how they contribute to their children's Early Years experience depending on family and work commitments, skills and personal preferences.

CASE STUDY

Parent Keira has worked with the administrator at her son's pre-school to write an application for a community grant which will enable them to re-surface the outdoor play area.

Parents John and Karen have teamed up with Nursery Nurses, Fatema and Gabriella, to take unwanted items from parents and staff members to the car boot sale to raise money for the children's trip to the zoo.

Parents Shipa, Tasha and Yvonne are working with the family involvement worker and the creche leader in their children's centre to produce story sacks. They are organising regular coffee mornings and lunchtime meetings for parents and staff members so that everybody can come and contribute ideas, time and labour.

Caretaker Ben has organised a working party of parents and staff to help clean up a neglected area of the school grounds on a Saturday morning. Over lunch they discuss and organise the work over the next few weeks to turn this area into the new wildlife garden.

Opening up opportunities for parents to contribute to the life of your setting has many advantages. For the setting it can save money or raise additional income, and premises and resources can be improved. Joint projects like the ones mentioned in the case study can create helpful publicity and raise your profile in the local community, particularly as positive experiences will lead parents to informally promoting your setting to friends and neighbours. For staff members the increased contact with the parents develops relationships with individual families and enhances their understanding of the local community. The additional time staff members have to contribute may be seen as a disadvantage but this needs to be balanced against the advantages for the setting and staff team and the many benefits for parents and children.

- Parents get to know staff members in a more informal environment which can help develop relationships.

- Parents develop self-esteem and become more confident.

- Parents get to know other parents which helps to reduce their feelings of isolation.

- Parents develop a sense of ownership of 'their' centre, pre-school or school which will motivate them to get involved further.

- Parents have the opportunity to develop their own skills, either practical, organisational or social.

- Children will benefit from a better physical environment.

- Children will see their parents modelling positive contributions to their community.

- Children will benefit from growing up in a neighbourhood with a strong sense of community.

Consider the opportunities parents currently have to participate in your setting. Do they encourage parents and staff to work together? Could joint working be improved?

Early Years practitioners and their settings are, like everybody else, grateful for a helping hand. To reap the benefits of partnership working it is important, though, not to create opportunities where parents complete some of the necessary and helpful tasks in isolation but to arrange their contributions in ways that also involve Early Years practitioners and other staff members. The interaction and the dialogue between parent and professional are key factors in partnership working.

Partnership working in leadership and management

In Chapter 2 you considered some misconceptions about parents, one of them being that parents are not interested in leadership roles. You read at that stage that many parents are already involved in the partnership boards of their children's centres, in nursery school governing bodies and in pre-school committees. In these roles they work with staff members from the setting, with a range of different professionals from the same geographical area and with other parents. In the case of governing bodies and pre-school committees, the roles and responsibilities of individual members and the group as a whole are clearly defined. In children's centres partnership boards are still at an early stage of development and there are a range of different approaches to leadership and governance. Many children's centre boards fulfil a more advisory role than governing bodies but draw members from a much more diverse group of people. Parents involved at this level have access to training programmes run by local governors support services, councils for voluntary services or other statutory and voluntary organisations. However, this type of involvement does not suit all parents and the number of parent representatives on these bodies or committees is normally small. To ensure that parental views are better represented and to increase the number of parents involved in management and leadership decisions, a different arrangement for parents to meet and comment may be helpful. This might be a parent forum, as suggested in the Sure Start Children's Centres Planning and Performance Management Guidance (Department for Education and Skills, 2006). Although this Guidance is aimed at children's centres, other Early Years settings, voluntary, statutory or private, may also find such a group beneficial.

The parent forum is an active working group for the setting, generally arranged in a series of meetings organised by the senior manager in the nursery, after consultation with parents.

- *To give parents a voice in the setting.*

- *To involve parents in the life of the setting.*

- *To ensure a free flow of communications between parents and staff.*

- *To support the social and personal development of parents and staff.*

- *To act as a link with the local community.*

- *To represent all parents within the nursery.*

(Pre-school Learning Alliance, 2008, p1)

The Pre-school Learning Alliance suggests a parent forum that includes staff members as well as parents, while some Sure Start Local Programmes have been working with parent forums entirely made up of parents with a facilitator as the only staff member attending. The latter allows the forum to be more strongly representative of the parents' view while the former gives the opportunity to bring staff members and parents closer together and develop their relationships. The exact membership should be discussed in each setting and a consensus found with the help of parents, staff members and managers. The aims of the forum will be similar in either case: enabling parents (and potentially staff members) to have a voice in the leadership and management of the Early Years setting, to contribute to important decisions for the setting, and to support individual members to develop their skills, either social, organisational, or personal.

Other tasks of the forum will be influenced by its relationship within the relevant leadership and management structure. In many children's centres and Sure Start Local Programmes parent forum members elect representatives who will speak for the forum and parents in general at partnership board and governors meetings. At the same time they are able to bring the views, concerns and issues from board meetings to the forum for a more detailed discussion.

CASE STUDY

At the children's centre partnership board meeting the manager invited members to participate in the recruitment process for the new family involvement worker. The board discussed who would be the best person to do this and decided that, because of the close relationship between this staff member and the families, it would be most beneficial if parents took part in the shortlisting and interview process. The board invited the forum to discuss this at their next meeting and arrange with the children's centre manager how their participation could be arranged. It was agreed at the forum meeting that three interested members were to join the shortlisting meeting (where an Early Years practitioner was available to care for and play with the children). On the day of the interviews parent forum members and their children met candidates informally as the first part of the interview to enable candidates to ask questions about the local area and for parents to gain an impression of how candidates related to parents and children. Candidates then met the formal interview panel which consisted of the manager, a senior practitioner and a parent board member. Afterwards there was a joined feedback session and it quickly became apparent who the most suitable candidate was for the family involvement worker post.

When parents participate at leadership and management level in an Early Years setting, it is more likely that the setting will deliver services which meet the families' needs. It also means that difficult decisions, for example about changes to services due to funding cuts, can be discussed and negotiated allowing families an element of control over the changes in their setting or community.

Earlier in this chapter you looked at ways in which parents and Early Years practitioners can work in partnership to enhance children's learning either in the setting or at home. This was focussed on relationships between one family and one staff member to agree the approach to an individual child's learning. The parent forum can be a venue for a wider discussion about the learning in the whole setting. In forum meetings parents and staff members can come together to consider and agree, for example, the ethos of the setting or its approach to learning and the curriculum.

REFLECTIVE TASK

Consider what your role as the Early Years Professional is in relation to parents and staff members when an Early Years setting wants to establish a parent forum.

FEEDBACK

Beyond the practical tasks of planning and facilitating meetings the Early Years Professional has a key role to play in encouraging parents and staff members to embrace the ethos of partnership working and to attend the forum. Creating a working environment where challenge and debate are welcome and modelling the effective participation in discussions and meetings are further elements of your role in this respect.

One of the cornerstones of good management and leadership is the ongoing development of services based on regular evaluation. For Early Years settings in the private, voluntary or independent sector there are strong business reasons to ensure that families as their clients are happy with their services, continue to use them and hopefully recommend them to others. In school, inspectors from the Office for Standards in Education talk to parents to establish whether families feel the school meets their needs and children's centres have to report annually on how satisfied families are with the services on offer to them. Collecting feedback on a regular basis and using it to develop and enhance services is therefore important for all Early Years practitioners. A parent forum may be well-placed to support this process as parents can judge best what the most effective methods of seeking feedback are, or how questions should be phrased to be clear and render useful information. In addition to designing the evaluation or feedback questions, parent forum members may also be ideally placed to carry out surveys and interviews as other parents are likely to find it easier to talk to them than to practitioners or other staff members they do not see very often; particularly if their comments are challenging. Parents may also know families in their community who have decided not to use your setting; the views of these families are particularly valuable for the planning and development of further services. Apart from the benefits for the setting as a whole, supporting parents to carry out evaluations can act as a very motivational factor as it develops the skills of individual parents, encourages them to work together as a group and enables them to take part in the development and leadership of their children's Early Years setting (see Chapter 7 for monitoring and evaluations).

Formalising partnership working

You have now explored in some detail how you can work in partnership with parents in your setting based on the development of trusting and supportive relationships. To work successfully in this way, it will be necessary to have wide support and gain a commitment to this approach from colleagues as well as from the management or leadership team and from the parents. Through discussions, reviews, evaluations, and consultations partnership working can be put into practice and consensus can be achieved on what forms it should take. To ensure this way of working becomes embedded it is also advisable to include it in the formal structure of the setting. A strong commitment to parental involvement and partnership working in your vision statement, aims or ethos will send a clear message to parents and the wider community that you are open to co-operating with others on equal terms. A separate policy on parental involvement will help parents and staff members alike to understand the importance of this way of working and their respective roles in it. This policy could also include the terms of reference for the parent forum in your setting clarifying its membership, role and responsibilities. Developing these together with staff members and parents will, in itself, contribute to the development of relationships. The following terms of reference for a parent forum in a Sure Start Children's Centre demonstrate how a parent forum could be embedded in the structure of a children's centre.

CASE STUDY

Who can join
All parents using services at or delivered by the Children's Centre are eligible to attend the Parent Forum. The Parent Forum Worker will attend all meetings but does not have the right to vote. Other children's centre staff and professionals can attend by invitation only.

How it works
The Forum acts as a voice for families using children's centre services. Members can discuss services and activities relating to the children's centre and issues arising from them. They can suggest new services, review and evaluate existing provision, and organise activities for Forum members, children's centre users and families in the wider community.

The Parent Forum meets once a month except in August. Meetings last two hours and are minuted. A crèche will be provided. The Parent Forum will elect its chair and

---

vice-chair in January each year for one year. This will be done by secret ballot with a simple majority.

The chair, vice-chair and the Parent Forum Worker agree the agenda. The chair leads the meetings. In his/her absence the vice-chair leads the meetings. Every member has one vote. The chair (or the vice-chair, in his/her absence) has the casting vote. Meetings will be quorate when seven members are present.

Liaison with the Children's Centre Partnership Board
The Forum works closely with the Partnership Board of the Children's Centre. Minutes from each Parent Forum meeting shall be available at each Board meeting and vice versa. The chair of the Partnership Board can request items to be added to the Parent Forum agenda and the Parent Forum chair can request items to be considered by the Partnership Board. The Parent Forum will elect two representatives for the Partnership Board by secret ballot from amongst their members. The parent representatives are to attend Parent Forum and Partnership Board meetings regularly and provide a link between Forum and Board (adapted from Sure Start Cambridge, 2007).

Building on the structures and processes outlined in your policies you can introduce the concepts of involvement and partnership working for the benefit of the child to parents when they first contact your setting. Relevant information can be included in prospectuses, parent leaflets and other publicity. The initiative for partnership working will normally rest with the staff team. It is therefore important for you in your leadership role to work with staff members to develop an appropriate concept together and encourage them to embrace the principle of partnership working. As the training and development of Early Years practitioners have a strong child-focus, it may be necessary to consider training opportunities to help staff members to develop their skills in working with parents. The National Occupational Standards for Work with Parents mentioned earlier may be a good tool for you to use in your team. In addition to encouraging practitioners to embrace partnership working with parents and formalising this approach in setting structures and policies, working arrangements also need to support this. Within staff rotas and shift patterns there needs to be time for Early Years practitioners to work with and talk to parents and premises should offer space away from the children for parents and staff members to talk quietly and confidentially.

C H A P T E R   S U M M A R Y

In this chapter we have looked at the practical aspects of involving parents in your Early Years setting and in their child's learning. Parental involvement has emerged as an ongoing process which requires the professional to constantly adjust and vary methods to meet the needs and preferences of parents. After the initial engagement with parents the building of trusting relationships becomes important and we explored some of the underlying principles for the interaction of Early Years practitioners with parents. Over time professionals and parents can develop partnership working in Early Years settings in a number of different spheres, to enhance children's learning, to support the setting as a whole and to contribute to leadership and management. Your responsibility as a leader of practice includes creating a working ethos and environment where colleagues feel able to embrace the work with parents and enabling parents to participate by creating a range of different involvement opportunities for them. We highlighted the benefits of formalising parental involvement by amending vision statements, policies and procedures in your setting and recognised the need to support Early Years practitioners with appropriate training in working with adults.

Self-assessment questions

1   What are the main features of an effective parenting course?

2   What are the main strengths and weaknesses of a parent forum which includes parents as well as staff members from the Early Years setting?

3   Explain the varying role of the Early Years practitioner in the continuum of access or process of engagement with services.

Moving on

In spite of a strong commitment to partnership working and parental involvement it is not always easy to engage with parents. In the next chapter you will analyse factors which act as barriers to involvement and consider strategies to overcome them, while Chapter 7 will critically assess difficulties in partnership working. In Chapter 6 you will have the opportunity to explore in more depth how adults learn and how you can offer effective learning opportunities for them. This chapter will also explore how professionals, parents and children can learn together. You may want to spend some time now reflecting on difficulties you have encountered in your work with parents and assess whether, with the new knowledge and understanding you have gained so far, you would already be able to approach similar challenging situations in a different way.

REFERENCES

Arnold, C (2008), Persistence pays off: working with parents who find our services 'hard to reach', in Whalley, M and the Pen Green Centre Team (ed) *Involving parents in their children's learning.* London: Paul Chapman Publishing.

Barlow, J, Kirkpatrick, S and Steward-Brown, S (2008), Parenting support in Sure Start, in Anning, A and Ball, M (eds) *Improving services for young children, from Sure Start to children's centres.*, London: SAGE Publications Ltd.

Collins English Dictionary 21st Century Edition (2001). Glasgow: HarperCollins Publishers.

Daycare Trust (2003) Focus on effective provision of pre-school education, *Partners,* 27: 6–7.

Department for Education and Skills (2006) Sure Start children's centres planning and performance management guidance, (**www.surestart.gov.uk** accessed on 15 January 2008).

Desforges, C and Abouchaar, A (2003), *The impact of parental involvement, parental support and family education on pupil achievements and adjustment: a literature review* (Research Report 443). Nottingham: DfES Publications.

Evangelou, M, Sylva, K, Edwards, A and Smith, T (2008), *Supporting parents in promoting early learning: the evaluation of the Early Learning Partnership Project*: DCSF Research Brief 039 (**www.dcsf.gov.uk/research/data/uploadfiles/DCSF-RB039A.pdf,** accessed on 20 October 2008).

Garbers, C, Tunstill, J, Allncok, D, and Akhurst, S (2006) Facilitating access to services for children and families: lessons from Sure Start local programmes, *Child and Family Social Work,* 11: 287–296.

Knopf, H and Swick, K (2007) How parents feel about their child's teacher/school: implications for early childhood professionals, *Early Childhood Education Journal,* 34(4): 291–296.

Pre-school Learning Alliance (2008) *Fact sheet: the parent forum,* (**www.pre-school.org.uk/resources/** accessed on 29 October 2008).

Rodd, J (2006) *Leadership in early childhood.* Maidenhead: Open University Press.

Siraj-Blatchford, I, Sylva, K, Muttock, S, Gilden, R, and Bell, D (2002), Researching effective pedagogy in the Early Years (Research Report RR356), Department of Educational Studies, University of Oxford. London: DfES.

Sure Start Cambridge (2007) Draft parent forum terms of reference, unpublished.

FURTHER READING

Knopf, H and Swick, K (2007) How parents feel about their child's teacher/school: implications for early childhood professionals, *Early Childhood Education Journal,* 34(4): 291–296.
This short journal article addresses perceptions regarding parents with young children and offers strategies for relationship building.

Whalley, M and the Pen Green Centre Team (2008) 2nd edition. *Involving parents in their children's learning.* London, Paul Chapman Publishing. (**www.pengreen.org**)
The Pen Green Centre models excellent practice in respect of working in partnership with parents and enhancing parents' understanding of children's learning. This book is of particular interest if you want to explore working with parents to enhance children's cognitive development.

USEFUL WEBSITES

www.openlearn.open.ac.uk/course/view.php?id=1539
Parents as partners learning module.

www.familylearning.org.uk
Information and activities to encourage families learning together.

www.peal.org.uk/
Information on how to involve parents in children's learning.

www.natcen.ac.uk/natcen/pages/or_familiesandchildren.htm
Offers recent research reports.

5 Partnership working: when parents are not in your setting

CHAPTER OBJECTIVES

After reading this chapter you should be able to:

- analyse the need to involve fathers, Black and Minority Ethnic groups and hard-to-reach families in your setting;
- critically assess approaches to working with fathers, Black and Minority Ethnic groups and hard-to-reach families;
- identify strategies to make your setting more accessible;
- examine the benefits of outreach work and joint working with other agencies and community groups to enhance the involvement of parents in Early Years settings.

This chapter develops your knowledge and understanding of how you can engage with parents and families who only rarely come into your setting or who do not access your services at all. The content is particularly relevant to 'S29', 'S30', 'S31', and 'S32' because these standards require you to reflect on your approach to working in partnership with all parents to enhance their children's learning. Furthermore, the chapter relates to 'S35', 'S38' and 'S39' as a better understanding of inhibiting and facilitating factors in relation to parental involvement will lead to improvements in your own practice while also helping you to influence the ethos and practice in your setting. Your learning in this chapter will extend your expertise in the following areas of the Common Core of Skills and Knowledge for the Children's Workforce; effective communication and engagement, multi-agency working, and sharing information.

Introduction

Some parents rarely come into your Early Years setting or take part in the activities you offer and some families do not access your services at all. These parents may be fathers or working mothers; the families may be from Black and Minority Ethnic groups or they may be described as hard-to-reach. Although it is easy to label parents with these terms it must be stressed that not all fathers hesitate to get engaged with their children's Early Years education, not all families from Black and Minority Ethnic groups are absent from your setting and so on. The groups in themselves are complex with different levels of and barriers to engagement; at the same time there are similarities between the groups making it possible to use the same approaches to encourage participation. In your setting there may be other groups of parents who do not engage with you but we fail to mention them here. Nonetheless, the approaches and strategies discussed in this chapter may still inform your work with them. Many parents will also belong to more than one of the groups discussed here, for example a Bangladeshi father. The broad categorisation employed here is merely for our convenience as we strive for understanding rather than a reflection of how parents should be perceived.

The chapter will start with looking at hard-to-reach families and hard-to-access services. Your awareness of barriers to involvement will be increased, and strategies to establish more accessible services will be developed. You will examine your work with parents from Black and Minority Ethnic groups, again with a focus on initial engagement, and then explore the role of fathers in children's Early Years experiences considering both initial engagement and ongoing involvement. Within each of the three sections particular approaches, barriers or facilitating factors will be highlighted. To avoid duplication they are not always repeated for each group but are often applicable across the range of the groups we are exploring.

Hard-to-reach or hard-to-access?

You have already read in earlier chapters how beneficial it is for children and their parents to be involved in Early Years settings. Research, and in particular longitudinal studies, confirms this but also shows benefits for society as a whole, partly on financial grounds. It appears that £7 can be saved on adult services for every £1 spent on Early Years provision (Sylva, 1999 quoted in Arnold, 2007). Furthermore, for most practitioners in the Early Years sector there are overwhelming moral reasons for the work with hard-to-reach families as there is a real passion for offering equal chances to all children in their community. However, there are often considerable barriers, some of which may lie with the families and their experiences or circumstances making them 'hard-to-reach'. On the other hand, some of the barriers originate in the services themselves making them 'hard-to-access'.

REFLECTIVE TASK

The term 'hard-to-reach' has been in use for many years now. How would you define this term? Who do you think belongs to this group?

FEEDBACK

Your answer is likely to include some of the following: teenage parents, single-parent families, refugees, migrant workers, Bangladeshi women, unemployed men, adults with learning difficulties, women experiencing domestic violence, and Muslim families. It is impossible to write a conclusive list because, depending on the wider community contexts and situations, who is seen to be hard-to-reach will vary. For example, some families may be hard-to-reach because of their faith and culture in a small market town where there are only very few of them but not in a big county town where there is, for example, an active community based around a faith centre.

To embrace the variety of contexts likely to be involved a broad and general definition of the term 'hard-to-reach' may serve us best, which can then be extended in the light of local circumstances. Hard-to-reach families or parents are those who are eligible to receive and use services but who, for whatever reason, are not involved (Coe *et al*, 2008). We should also clarify what is meant by the term 'hard-to-access' which in line with the above definition, can mean those services which families and parents are eligible to receive but which, for whatever reason, they do not use.

PRACTICAL TASK

Go back to Chapter 3 where you looked at local demographic data and try to identify the hard-to-reach families in your area. Compare the statistics with your own monitoring data. Is your setting a service that families find hard-to-access?

FEEDBACK

As we are exploring who is not using your services and why not, it is important to have relevant monitoring data. Do you collect information on who comes to your play sessions, which parents come to consultations, who accompanies children on outings and so on? Good monitoring data will be able to tell you who engages with you and where there are problems in building relationships with families.

There are numerous barriers between families and services which prevent access and engagement, some originating in the services and some in the families. In the following sections you will focus on how you can address some of the barriers inside your setting, but also how you can support families to overcome some of their internal barriers.

Accessibility

In Chapter 3 you looked at parents' views of services, and how they wanted them to be delivered. Parents want services to be convenient and to meet the needs they identify for themselves. Convenience includes some of the practical aspects of an Early Years provision, be it day nursery sessions, play activities or pre-school outings. The timing needs to suit families and may depend on the start and finish time of the local primary school, the shift pattern at a local factory employing many parents, or the dates for different religious festivals. It is difficult for practitioners to be mindful of all relevant aspects but regular consultation and dialogue with parents will ensure that suitable timings can be arranged. To meet the requirements of families it may be necessary to be more flexible in the working times and shift patterns for Early Years practitioners, and some renegotiations may be necessary within teams.

The availability of a crèche or other forms of additional childcare is often described as helpful when trying to involve parents in meetings, courses, and volunteering opportunities. If you offer part-time care and education for children, parents will only be able to attend during the hours their child is in your setting and provided they have no younger children. Arranging a crèche to run alongside a course will allow more parents to attend. In some settings it may also be possible to accommodate additional children in some sessions on a short-term basis. Although the crèche or additional childcare will be arranged to enable parents to participate in an activity, it is important to ensure that the provision made for the children is appropriate for their ages and meets a high standard of care.

A further aspect of accessibility of services is their location. Within communities there are often natural boundaries – some families may not cross from one housing estate into another, a busy road may act as a barrier, or the distance may simply be too far for a mother with a double-buggy and another child walking. Parents' views of acceptable distances will vary greatly, and you will need to explore these with them. To get a comprehensive picture it will be important to collect the views of those families currently not using your setting as they are likely to be the ones who find the distance too great. To address the problem of geographical barriers you may want to consider providing transport for families or running sessions in different venues.

CASE STUDY

One and half miles from the new children's centre there is a large travellers' site. Access by car or on foot is only possible along one road cutting across a railway line. At the far end of the site there are a number of very old chalets, some of them in a poor state of repair, where 12 families from four different Eastern European countries live. The children's centre outreach worker and an interpreter had visited the site on several occasions to explain what a children's centre is and to invite families to play sessions but nobody followed the invitation and visited the centre. Some of the mothers explained to the interpreter that the centre was just too far away for them, especially as they had no car and would have to walk the distance. With one child in a pushchair that would be hard work but possible. For families with two or more children it simply seemed too much. In co-operation with other agencies the children's centre has been able to hire and staff a converted double-decker bus to offer detached work. Every other week the migrant families are now able to access advice and information and children have the opportunity to play and learn when the bus comes down their road.

FEEDBACK

Offering drop-ins, toddler groups, and workshops in venues other than your main base may be a good way of meeting families closer to their own homes, in premises they already know and where they feel comfortable. This can provide the initial contact point for families to get to know you and for you to develop your relationship with them. Once your service gets known and trust grows, families will find it easier to overcome distance and other barriers to participation and start using your main building and core service.

In addition to the geographical aspect accessibility has other dimensions, for example the welcome parents receive when they first approach a setting or services and the attitudes towards them from staff members and existing users. Parents sometimes experience professionals as not being very understanding, or as not paying attention to their needs; they do not feel they are being listened to and they are made to feel like bad parents (Quinton 2004). The attitude of some staff members in some services has been described as off-putting and patronising, and at the same time parents are afraid to be judged as being unable to cope (ATD Fourth World, 2006). This highlights the need to explore communication and interpersonal skills in Early Years settings to ensure they reflect values which are based on respect for others and principles which are grounded in anti-discriminatory practice. The suggestions for the development of good relationships with parents in Chapter 4 and the tasks in Chapter 2 exploring underlying attitudes to parents may offer you tools to work with individual team members. Regular staff training and discussions about ethos and values can also support the development of better approaches to parents and of positive and trusting relationships with them.

Existing users also play a vital role in the welcome new families receive in an Early Years setting, children's centre or play session. In children's centres, most families initially access services for the benefit of their child but, ongoing attendance is often motivated by the benefits to the parent. The adult enjoys meeting others, forms new friendships, and develops social networks. Soon their main motivation for joining courses and activities changes from learning for the child or developing new skills for themselves to socialising and meeting their friends. These users experience the centre as friendly and welcoming but, at the same time they shape an unexpressed culture for the centre with some implicit views of who may or may not fit in or who is or is not the 'right' person to join. Newcomers may subconsciously be expected to conform to these unwritten norms which creates an air of exclusivity and may make the centre (or its users) appear less welcoming. Consequently, the families who would most benefit from the services of the centre may feel excluded and unable to access them (Sheppard *et al*, 2008). Unexpressed cultures can also develop in pre-schools or nurseries where users encourage friends to join the setting but little promotion is done in the wider community which leads to new families belonging to the same social group or community as existing ones.

REFLECTIVE TASK

Think about the families in your setting. Do you think there is a specific hidden culture? How welcoming and accessible is your setting to newcomers? Are existing users acting as gatekeepers inadvertently stopping others from using your services?

FEEDBACK

Service users can be a powerful and positive force in an Early Years setting; however, practitioners need to be aware that existing users can also have a detrimental impact if they bring discrimination, stereotypes and prejudices into the setting. Practitioners need to be clear about the values and ethos of the setting so that they can model and reflect these to all users and, if need be, proactively challenge discrimination and widen participation.

Isolation

If a friend already uses a pre-school or children's centre, then a parent will find it easier to access this service as well. However, many hard-to-reach families are socially isolated and do not necessarily have good links in their local community. Offering outreach or detached services will therefore be an effective approach to engaging with them.

CASE STUDY

The doorstep library
ATD Fourth World developed a pilot doorstep library on a housing estate in Southward, south London. The estate houses a community with the reputation of being hard to reach. The doorstep library actively involved around 80 children and their families, proving to be a very positive way to engage with disadvantaged families.

The first step, in July 2004, was to set up an outdoor library running once a week for two hours. Blankets were spread out on the green area in front of a block of flats, with books and simple activities, such as colouring or musical instruments. The doorstep library team (workers and volunteers) knocked on all the doors in the building and invited parents and children to join the library. Some of the more outgoing families – those who were less excluded – had the confidence to join in the activities. Other families saw the library taking place and, bit by bit, became familiar with it.

After six months, the doorstep library started to take books around the flats, offering to read to the children or to lend some books. People were always free to say no . . . After a year, 43 families had borrowed books and children from 25 families had taken part in home reading sessions.

CASE STUDY *continued*

Nearly a year after it started, the doorstep library organised a six-day summer festival on the estate, gathering ideas from each family and giving support to parents and neighbours in preparing and running activities . . .

A year and a half into the project, the doorstep library team has been able to develop a relationship with more than 50 families living on the estate. Through regular weekly contact, parents have gained the confidence to share their difficulties and strengths and the doorstep library team has helped some of them to make use of local services.

(ATD Fourth World, 2006, p2)

FEEDBACK

Taking services to families' homes is an effective way to overcome isolation. The example of the doorstep library also demonstrates the time and perseverance required to engage with some hard-to-reach families as it takes many months to get your service known in the community and to gain trust. Short-term pilot and engagement projects may therefore not always be very successful.

Further barriers to parents' engagement in their children's Early Years experiences may arise from poor experiences during their own school days, and a general lack of confidence and self esteem. Parents may be fearful about professionals whom they perceive as authority figures; there may be feelings of anger related to previous incidences when services did not meet their needs; and parents may be anxious because they do not know how Early Years education works and what will be expected of them and their children. Consequently, parents may be reluctant to use a nursery or pre-school at all, or, if they have decided to bring their child to your setting, they may not engage in dialogue with you or in any activities you offer for parents or families. Arnold (2007) describes practical ways of overcoming the barriers to engagement based on personal feelings.

> *Often parents are anxious and lack confidence. If we **accept them** and their children and genuinely like them, parents will begin to loosen up. We must always **be scrupulously** fair, and sometimes this involves **explaining our decisions** and policies to parents. They have a right to know how decisions are made. Whenever possible, we can **involve them in the decision-making process**. We always try to **listen** to complaints and apologise if we are in the wrong.*

> *It is important to **acknowledge feelings**, the parents' and their child's. Often something quite small can make the parents angry . . .*

> *We **offer one-to-one support** if parents are shy or lack confidence in a group situation . . .*

> Sometimes **parents need convincing that they and their child have potential**. We closely observe children, and our observations are invaluable information to pass on to parents on a daily basis if possible. This can alert the parent to specific things to watch out for at home and to share with us.
>
> We often **reflect back to parents the major role we see them playing** in their child's development and learning.
>
> (Arnold, 2007, pp100–101) (Emphasis author's own)

In order to enable parents to participate and get involved in your setting, you have to acknowledge their feelings and accept them as the starting point for your work with this family. Only then can you build a relationship with them and engage with them in the dialogue about the child's learning and development.

Appropriate information

Evaluations of the engagement of hard-to-reach families in Sure Start Local Programmes have pointed to a further obstacle to participation: the lack of timely and appropriate information (Coe *et al*, 2008). Many non-users thought the services were not for them or did not know about them at all. This raises important questions about how Early Years settings advertise their services. We discussed earlier that word-of-mouth is an important way of letting parents know about your provision. This may, however, only address a limited audience and not reach those most in need of your provision. Written information may not be accessible to all due to literacy or language barriers. We have already mentioned improving accessibility through outreach work (case study: the doorstep library). By visiting toddler groups or taking part in community events you can introduce yourself to parents and inform them about your provision explaining what you do and what services families can access in your setting. Employing an outreach worker may also be an effective strategy to engage with more families as he can clarify misconceptions about your setting in the community and help families overcome their anxieties about coming to a provision where they do not know anybody.

The lack of clear and appropriate information is often an issue at the initial engagement stage but can also cause problems when families are already using your setting. Information about outings or handouts giving details of the curriculum may not be read by everybody and you may need to consider talking individual parents through any written material or providing translations into the relevant community languages. Information may also need to be given several times before parents act on it. As explored earlier, involvement is a process and at different stages there may be different problems. It is worth monitoring parents' engagement with children's learning and parental participation in other activities so that you are alerted early to any changes and can address them effectively, for example by sharing important information face-to-face rather than relying on a letter or handout.

Black and Minority Ethnic groups

At the start of the chapter you looked at which families may be hard-to-reach and it is highly likely that you included families from different ethnic groups. Belonging to a Black and Minority Ethnic (BME) group does not automatically mean a family is hard-to-reach though; there is great variety in, for example, needs and vulnerability, educational attainment, income, and aspirations for their children. However, statistically a higher number of BME families than White British families experience poverty and ill-health. Their housing is generally poorer, their income is lower and their unemployment rates higher. BME families seem to face particular barriers which prevent them from accessing childcare although there is a demand for it (Lloyd and Rafferty, 2006). The educational attainment of children from different BME groups shows some considerable variation. However, Desforges and Abouchaar (2003) argue that the level of children's achievement is not first and foremost influenced by their ethnicity but by socio-economic factors. Parental aspirations have also been shown to have a major impact across different ethnic groups; if parents' aspirations for their children are high, then children will achieve better outcomes at school. This highlights the need for practitioners to engage BME parents in their children's Early Years settings so that they can raise parental expectations and support them to further their children's learning.

As with the term 'hard-to-reach' a conclusive definition of BME groups is difficult, but the understanding of the term BME as being *used to describe people experiencing racial discrimination because of their skin colour, their ethnicity, their culture, or for other connected reasons* (Pascal and Bertram, 2004, cited in Lloyd and Rafferty, 2006, p7) seems adequate for our reflections on the work with parents. In many communities this definition will include Travellers, migrant workers, asylum seekers and refugees. As mentioned above, it is helpful to look at population figures to establish which minority groups live in your area. This will enable you to plan and prepare your work with them.

Although BME families may face similar barriers to the ones we discussed above for hard-to-reach groups there are further factors which may make access to services difficult for them.

REFLECTIVE TASK

What do you think are the barriers BME families have to overcome to access your setting?

FEEDBACK

You may have identified some of the following barriers: parents do not speak English, parents are not familiar with the British Early Years education system, they think services are not for them, there are concerns that other members of their community may regard them as bad parents if they do not look after their children themselves, lack of trust, anxiety about whether their faith-based and cultural needs and values will be respected, and not knowing anybody in the setting.

There are different approaches and strategies, in addition to the ones mentioned above, to help BME families overcome barriers to involvement, for example working with ambassadors from the BME groups, involving BME families in consultation, employing staff from BME groups, and working with partners from other agencies and organisations. These will be explored in the next four sections with a brief explanation of which barriers they could overcome and how you can employ them in your setting.

Community ambassadors

Working closely with one person from a BME group, developing good relationships with her and making her your ambassador or champion may help you gain acceptance in her community. As the ambassador speaks the community language, she can overcome linguistic barriers and explain culturally different parameters more sensitively. BME families will be encouraged by seeing somebody from their community using and recommending your Early Years setting and the ambassador can support them to access your services.

CASE STUDY

After discussions with the City Council Development Worker for the Bangladeshi community the children's centre started to run a Bangladeshi Family Play Session. A flyer was produced and translated and then distributed by the Development Worker and by children's centre staff. The initial take-up was poor, only two families attended over a period of a month. This, however, gave staff the opportunity to talk in detail to the mothers about the benefits of play and their children's development. One of the mothers, Selma, became very enthusiastic about the session, especially as she saw how much her sons were enjoying themselves. She felt strongly that the play session should benefit more children in her community. She spoke to the session leader and together they redesigned the flyer to give more information on what parents could expect when they came. Selma used the flyer to talk to some of her friends and neighbours and invited them to come along. If they were unsure about coming, Selma arranged to meet with them and walk to the centre with them. Other families she rang the day before the sessions to remind them it was happening. She welcomed families to the sessions with the session leader and interpreted when that was needed. Through her ongoing support for the session and her willingness to talk to her community about it more families started to attend giving children access to good quality play and parents an understanding of the value of play to support their children's learning.

The process of one parent encouraging another to use services happens quite naturally but you may wish to formalise this by offering additional support to the parent ambassador to understand your services better, develop communication skills, and be aware of other BME families outside her immediate friendship or family group. Working closely with your community ambassador and offering appropriate training and support will enable you to avoid the ambassador becoming gatekeeper to your services. An ambassador who can also help you by interpreting and translating is invaluable although you may need to consider whether it is always appropriate to have a neighbour or friend interpret, for example when you have to address sensitive issues about a child's home life.

Finding a BME community member who is interested in working with you is not always easy. This could be a parent who is already using your services and becomes very motivated by her own experiences but you may also have to actively look for a suitable person. For the work with some BME groups faith organisations are good partners to liaise with. If faith leaders endorse your setting, there will be a wider understanding that the services you offer are for them and community members will find it more acceptable to use them. In some BME groups you may want to address the father in the first instance and gain his acceptance before working with his family. As the work of the ambassador is focussed on her specific community there will be a need for you to find different ambassadors for the various BME groups in your area. Although you and your staff team may have to invest a considerable amount of time into developing and working with ambassadors, the increased engagement of minority groups in your setting and the benefits for the children in your neighbourhood will be substantial.

Consultation

Engaging with the BME groups in your area as early as possible when you plan to develop a new Early Years setting, expand your provision or start a new project will be beneficial and community ambassadors can support you in this. Seeking the views of minority groups as part of the consultation process will help families understand that the services you are going to offer are intended for them and will give you an early opportunity to let families know about your setting. A thorough consultation process will enable you to ensure that services can be set up to meet the needs of local families which in turn will mean that there will be good take-up. Ongoing consultation and evaluation with BME groups and the whole community will ensure that services continue to meet local needs by making you aware of and able to respond to changes in the community.

Recruitment to staff and leadership teams

To help you and your team overcome language barriers you may consider employing a staff member from a BME group. In addition to making daily conversations with children and parents easier, this will bring an understanding of the culture directly into your setting. The BME staff member can support practitioners to develop their knowledge of an ethnic group and introduce more culturally sensitive work practices. However, because your staff member comes from a local BME group and speaks the 'right' language, this does not necessarily means he shares the same faith or cultural background as your whole BME community. There is great diversity within different BME groups and there are, of course, personal differences between individuals. Recruiting a BME member to your team is a helpful tool to overcome some barriers but should be seen to be a starting point for the exploration of cultural and ethnic issues within your team and your setting rather than the ultimate solution to all problems regarding the engagement with BME families. The BME staff member should not be the only one working with families from a Minority Ethnic group as this re-enforces separation. He should work across ethnic and cultural boundaries together with all other staff members and by doing so enhance the understanding between different ethnic groups in your setting and in the wider community.

Notwithstanding potential issues arising from how BME staff members are deployed in your setting, their presence will provide positive images and role models to the community. A further approach to showing BME families that you value them is recruiting board or committee members from their communities. You have already explored the importance of parental involvement in the leadership of an Early Years setting and the support parents may need to fulfil these roles. Because of language barriers and different cultural expectations members of BME groups may need additional support and you may not be able to fill the board or committee vacancies immediately. You may have to be prepared to wait until you have developed strong and trusting relationships and individual community members are ready to join your setting.

Multi-agency working

We have already suggested that it is helpful to work in co-operation with others when trying to engage with BME groups, be it community ambassadors or staff and board members from the BME communities. There is a range of other services working with and for BME families, some linked to local authorities, others from the voluntary sector, for example the race equality and diversity service of your local authority, community development officers, a Travellers' education service, and a Black Minority Ethnic Forum. Developing the link with these agencies and their professionals will enable you to find support for your work with BME groups, as they are likely to know community leaders and members well and they have an understanding of the needs in the BME communities. A multi-agency approach to your initial engagement work with BME groups will also have long-term benefits: if families face particular problems which fall outside your remit and scope, you can signpost them effectively to other agencies who can help, for example to claim benefits, access language classes, or get legal advice on gaining citizenship. Working closely with other agencies with experience of the culture, ethos and values of BME groups can also provide a development opportunity for you and other practitioners as informal discussions and joint project work can be as effective as formal training in raising the awareness and understanding of other faiths, cultures and lifestyles.

PRACTICAL TASK

Go back to your response to the reflective task above relating to BME families. Can you see some strategies or approaches now which you could use to help BME families access your service?

FEEDBACK

In addition to the strategies already mentioned there are still many others you could try.

- *Offering targeted services for specific groups either in your setting or as outreach projects. This may help less confident families to access your services in the first instance. There needs to be an emphasis, though, on moving families on into mainstream services as soon as possible to avoid segregation and enhance community cohesion.*

FEEDBACK continued

- *Develop good monitoring practices so that you have a clear understanding of who accesses your services and how. This will help you to identify sections of the community not using your services or changes in use. It may also show you what works well with a particular BME group so that you can duplicate effective strategies in your work with other groups.*

- *Use translators so that you are able to offer your written information material in the relevant community languages.*

- *Develop a comprehensive training programme for staff members so that all of them increase their cultural awareness and can work comfortably and effectively across different ethnic and cultural boundaries.*

- *Use and display culturally sensitive resources, not just in the children's classrooms and play areas but also where parents, families and staff members meet.*

- *Stimulate an interest in and curiosity about different cultures in the parents as well as the children (maybe with a workshop on childrearing practices around the world).*

(For some of these suggestions see Craig, 2007)

Fathers and male carers

Earlier in this book we defined the term 'parents' as including mothers, fathers, guardians, carers and other significant adults in a child's life. Consequently, when we use the term 'fathers' in this chapter it should be understood to include biological fathers, step-fathers, mothers' new partners, grandfathers, older brothers, uncles and male foster carers. As society is changing the role of fathers is also evolving. With more second marriages, higher divorce rates, more women in employment, and greater flexibility in working hours, fathers are getting more involved in the Early Years experiences of their children. In fact, *today's dads undertake 800% more care of their infants and young children than their own fathers did* (O'Brien, 2004 quoted in Burgess, 2008, p1). This is a significant change in just one generation. However, in spite of this improvement and a strong emphasis in research and theory on the need to include fathers in their children's learning and development, in practice there is still only a minority of fathers actively engaged in Early Years settings.

You have considered the impact and interrelatedness of parent and Early Years Professional in relation to a child's learning in earlier chapters. At that stage you looked at 'parents' in general without discerning between mothers and fathers. However, there are some specific benefits arising from fathers' involvement in their children's lives in addition to the benefits the support from mothers brings:

Positive father involvement in their children's learning is associated with better education, social and emotional outcomes for children, including:

- *better examination results;*

- *better school attendance and behaviour;*

63

- *less criminality;*

- *higher quality of later relationships;*

- *better mental health.*

(Department for Education and Skills, 2004, p5)

As far as the motivation to get involved in their children's learning is concerned, it arises out of the love most fathers, like most mothers, have for their children and their desire to develop positive, supportive relationships with them so that they can help them to succeed and do well in their lives. In addition, fathers are often motivated by the children themselves, their interests and their encouragement to the fathers to join in. Statistically speaking, fathers are more likely to get involved if the mother is also taking a strong interest in the child's learning and development. Engagement is better when fathers live with their children and, in families where father and child live apart, when there is a good relationship between both parents. Lone fathers are also more likely to get involved and support their children's development (Department for Education and Skills, 2004).

When fathers support their children's learning and development they generally use the same pedagogical methods and strategies mothers apply and see themselves as the first educators or teachers of their children. However, mothers and fathers have a different understanding of their own learning alongside the child's: mothers believe that their own knowledge and understanding can be challenged and extended when they support their children, while fathers do not see themselves in the role of learners in the context of their child's development (Whalley and Chandler, 2007). Further aspects of adults as learners in Early Years settings and how you can support them will be explored in the next chapter.

CASE STUDY

John and his family registered with their Sure Start Local Programme in November 2003. For many months only his wife and children attended sessions (John has a full-time job) but when an after school play session started the following autumn, John came along with his family. Bev, the fathers' worker, got to know him as rather a shy man who held his head down most of the time making no eye contact. When a first aid course for fathers was offered, Bev and his wife persuaded John to join in. He attended all sessions but stayed very quiet most of the time. Towards the end of the course Bev encouraged fathers to think about other activities they may be interested in. John was keen to take his children to the zoo and suggested this. He met with Bev and another father after a course session to research different possibilities. He has since then attended further activities for fathers and their children (trip to soft play barn, outing to Fire Station, family visit to Santa's grotto at a garden centre for Christmas). In the following year he attended a parenting course for fathers. He is now much more relaxed and less shy when with other people, and has started encouraging other fathers to come to activities organised by the Sure Start Local Programme.

FEEDBACK

> *Fathers benefit in similar ways from involvement in their children's Early Years education as mothers do: their confidence and self-esteem grow and their social skills develop. Through organising events and activities they have the opportunity to learn new practical skills (see Chapter 1).*

You have already looked at a wide range of reasons why parents in general or parents from minority or hard-to-reach groups may not get involved in their children's early learning. These apply to fathers as much as they do to mothers; however, there are some specific barriers to fathers' involvement:

- work commitments;
- the perceived need to conform to male norms of behaviour;
- reluctance to seek advice;
- services are insensitive to fathers' needs;
- self-exclusion as fathers see themselves first and foremost in their economic role as providers rather than active educators;
- all female environment which re-enforces traditional roles;
- staff not considering the important role fathers play in their children's lives;
- staff not challenging mothers to involve fathers;
- view that men are a threat to children;
- view of men as perpetrators of domestic violence.

Most of these barriers are related to attitudes to fathers and you will have the opportunity to consider possible ways to overcome these later in this chapter. Firstly, you are going to explore some of the more practical issues regarding the work with fathers, that is to say the type of activities they may be interested in and how you can make initial contact with them.

Activities for fathers

The question of timing is always a very important one when trying to engage with families and preferences will vary greatly. When working fathers and mothers drop children off in the morning they may not have the time for a chat with staff as they will need to get to work; the afternoons are likely to be better. If you want working parents to attend an event during the day time, for example an outing, then you will have to plan well in advance so that they have the opportunity to arrange for leave, if that is possible at all. For working parents you will also have to consider offering activities, like workshops or courses, either towards the end of the afternoon or in the evening, or, if more time is required, arrange weekend sessions. The best way to approach this is to talk to your fathers and mothers about what timing may be best for them. In addition, you have to be prepared to run the same activity or event at two or even three different times to enable all parents to attend.

Your aim for the engagement with fathers will be to involve them in their children's learning and in the life of your Early Years setting, as discussed previously. To facilitate the initial engagement you may want to consider activities which have a particular appeal for fathers. In general, fathers seem more likely to attend one-off events or come to parent evenings than volunteer to help during pre-school or nursery sessions or join a committee (Kahn, 2006). They prefer activity-based sessions rather than discussion groups; a practical focus involving shared experiences with their children seems to be more attractive than a learning focus. Areas of interest are diverse, though, and can include ICT, arts, music, technology, sport, and drama. Programmes and activities that have been more successful are normally well planned and well structured, delivered in a dynamic way, and developed in consultation with fathers regarding timing, content, publicity, and design (NESS, 2003). Offering activities or courses exclusively for fathers can be very effective as this gives fathers the opportunity to engage with others in the more dynamic and activity-based style that many of them prefer. In addition, this enables them to develop social networks and discuss their particular approaches to parenting more freely. Although targeted services can help to build trust and develop initial relationships, it is important to encourage fathers to use universal services as soon as possible to avoid further segregation.

Early engagement

In addition to specific activities there are other factors which support the engagement of fathers. A greater presence of men in Early Years settings be they staff members, volunteers or students, gives fathers appropriate role models for their involvement with their children. A staff member with particular responsibility for the work with fathers will also demonstrate how much you value the input from fathers and gives their cause a champion within the setting. This worker will be able to be their contact point and develop trusting relationships with them. Interestingly, experience shows that this worker does not necessarily need to be a man – it is a question of work focus and commitment rather than one of the worker's gender. The right choice of language is another relevant factor in the engagement process. If you advertise an event for 'parents', this is often understood to mean 'mothers' rather than 'mothers and fathers'. Explicitly addressing mothers *and* fathers will help clarify that both parents are invited and will show that you are specifically interested in fathers getting involved in your setting (Kahn, 2005). Talking to mothers to stress that fathers are included in invitations and using them to specifically encourage their partners to come to events at your setting is a further strategy to employ when trying to engage with fathers. Research about fathers' involvement in Sure Start Local Programmes confirms that it is often the mother who influences the father and encourages the initial contact with services:

> *One father who was initially reluctant to get involved in a fathers' group but became involved after being encouraged to do so by his partner and now uses the Sure Start centre on a daily basis commented:*

I'm always sort of encouraged to come to these things . . . um . . . so I mean, Tracey's always collaring me . . . When I first started coming I didn't really want to come. It was only the effect of my partner basically dragging me up here that I came up . . . I didn't want to keep coming up here every time she was asking me to come up here. But now I don't even think about it . . . Just sort of got used to it sort of thing.

(NESS, 2003, p48)

Involvement in children's learning

In Chapter 4 you looked at different ways of sharing information with parents to support children's learning in the Early Years setting and in the home environment. Many of the methods discussed are suitable for fathers (or mothers) to use at home when they cannot come into your Early Years setting regularly. For example, following on from a workshop on children's learning your suggestions in the home-school diary can prompt a father to observe his child during a particular play activity. He could even video his child and he or the mother could use the footage for a discussion with the Early Years practitioner during the next consultation. After your discussion with the mother, who came to the parent evening, you can send a hand-out home for the father to explain one of the concepts you discussed and follow this up with a phone call to the father to offer further support in putting the suggested play strategies into practice at home. Many mothers and fathers would welcome email contact with their children's key workers to exchange observations or raise concerns. This shows that mothers and fathers do not have to come into the Early Years setting on a daily basis to be involved in their children's learning.

The suggestions made here for sharing information and working in partnership with mothers and fathers assume that good relationships exist already. Mothers and fathers are normally open to new learning during transition stages in their lives; in this case their child's start at nursery or pre-school, and you may want to consider how you can best use this short window of opportunity. We have already mentioned the importance of gathering good data to inform your work and you may want to review how much you currently know about the working or the non-resident parent. During home visits you can sensitively ask a range of questions and agree with mothers and/or fathers how you will communicate with each other and also negotiate whether communication will be possible with the non-resident parent. Offering parent workshops and information sessions during the first few weeks of a child starting in your setting may also provide a good environment for you to develop trusting relationships on which you can then build later on with less direct ways of communication. The main factor is to be flexible and try to accommodate the specific preferences and needs of individual families or family members.

Attitudes towards fathers in Early Years settings

Attitudes towards fathers play an important part in how well Early Years practitioners engage with them. As they are not seen very often in Early Years settings it is easy enough to forget fathers and work only with the mothers who come regularly. However, fathers' contributions to their children's well-being and development are so substantial, regardless of whether they live with their children or not, that professionals have to do their utmost to make them part of their children's early childhoods. The majority of Early Years practitioners are keen to engage with fathers because of the valuable contribution they make (Kahn, 2005 and 2006) and there is a general understanding that fathers love their children as much as mothers do. Occasionally, however, concerns are expressed that fathers may present a risk in relation to safeguarding children or may be potential perpetrators of domestic violence (NESS, 2003), which could then lead to fathers not being welcome in a setting. It is important to realise that the vast majority of men are neither a risk to children nor to women, and a potential threat from a very small number of men should not hamper the crucial work of engaging fathers in their children's learning.

In addition to the attitudes of others, fathers' own attitudes may present barriers for their engagement with Early Years settings. You have already read that many fathers do not feel invited if you address a letter to 'parents' and they often think (in line with some other hard-to-reach groups) that services are not intended for them. In addition, they may feel the need to conform to male stereotypes and male norms of behaviour, which represent men as earning a living and providing for the family in economic terms rather than portray fathers as caring for babies or taking toddlers to play sessions. Many fathers assume that the main responsibility for bringing up children rests with the mother and they see themselves as supporting their partners in this role rather than taking part on equal terms. How individual fathers see and understand their role in their children's lives needs exploring to support them to understand the important contribution they make. Mothers' attitudes to fathers' involvement may also need to be challenged. Discussions with parents at the Pen Green Centre show that both mothers and fathers make assumptions about their partners' views on fathers' involvement.

> *In our discussions with parents, mothers initially assumed that their partners did not want to be involved, and the fathers assumed that their partners did not want them to be involved. In the vast majority of cases, these assumptions were not well founded.*
>
> (Whalley and Chandler, 2007, p77)

This highlights the need to consult with mothers *and* fathers about involvement but also to discuss gender issues with them, for example gender-specific roles, gender stereotyping, and the separate and joint contributions mothers and fathers make to children's well-being and development.

REFLECTIVE TASK

Consider the different views that mothers and fathers have in respect of fathers' involvement in their children's Early Years experiences. Have you encountered anything similar in the families in your setting? Are gender issues discussed in your staff team at all?

FEEDBACK

Research has shown that in settings where staff members are aware of and discuss gender issues, parents also discuss gender matters (Kahn, 2006) which suggests that staff members have to take the initiative with the gender discussion. Through dialogue mothers and fathers can be encouraged to reflect on stereotypes, understand each other's views better and agree on more evenly balanced contributions to their children's development and learning.

In relation to fathers you have looked at what type of activities they may choose to get involved in and how these should be timed and organised. You looked at ways to involve them even if they do not regularly come into your setting and considered the need to address and discuss gender issues as this can help overcome many of the barriers to fathers' involvement listed earlier in this section. Many of the strategies discussed with reference to hard-to-reach groups and BME groups are also relevant to fathers and will help you in your attempts to engage with them, for example offering detached work, consulting thoroughly when developing services, and working with a community ambassador to let fathers know about your setting. To a very large extent the success of your work with fathers (and minority groups) will depend on the commitment you and your team make to them. This dedication to working with fathers can be developed through discussions in the staff team and through training. Both can be directly related to fathers and men or related to the wider questions of diversity and equality, challenging prejudice, and establishing anti-discriminatory practice. Changing policies, terms of reference and vision statements for your setting will also help to embed the importance of fathers in your work with children.

PRACTICAL TASK

Write a strategy or action plan to help you bring about change in your setting's work with fathers. Who needs to be involved? What needs to be different? How can attitudes and procedures be changed?

FEEDBACK

Your action plan may include some of the following steps.

- *Review existing data: what information do you collect on fathers, especially non-resident fathers? It may be useful to have details of fathers' shift patterns, their particular interests, or their preferred language. If you do not regularly monitor who comes into your setting, you may want to note for one or two weeks who drops children off, which parent (mother or father) responds to requests for help, or who rings to ask about a place at the nursery, to see how many fathers are already in contact with you. Collecting and monitoring data will give you useful information when deciding on how to structure your work with fathers and help you evaluate later on which activities or approaches work and which are less successful.*

- *Audit skills and experience in the team: staff members who have worked with men before could share their experiences. Others may be able to cascade relevant messages and ideas from recent training. An audit may highlight the need for additional training for the whole team.*

- *Start gender discussions in your team: this could happen in a team meeting if it gives enough time or you may want to organise a special event. It will be important to have a whole-setting approach to bring about significant change for all your families. The starting point could be the discussion of an incident between children in your pre-school or an article from a local newspaper which relates to gender issues. Governors, trustees and committee members should also be included in these discussions. This could happen at their separate meetings or you could organise an away-day for staff, board and committee members so that everybody involved in the setting can contribute to the discussion and to the development of a new way of working.*

- *Consult with fathers: especially with those you do not currently meet in your setting. Find out what they are interested in, what is important to them about their children and their Early Years setting, how and when they could get involved and so on. To be successful your work with fathers needs to be in response to their needs and their preferences. Once relationships have been established you will be able to introduce other topics or ways of involvement that did not initially seem relevant to fathers.*

- *Start gender discussions with mothers and fathers: once staff members have had time to reflect on gender issues and feel more confident about the subject, encourage the wider discussion about gender issues. You could organise a workshop or invite a relevant speaker to a regular session you already run for families or include gender issues in your conversations at drop-off and pick-up time. In the home-school diary you can prompt mothers and fathers to observe their children's play and detect gender stereotypes. Explore up to which extent mothers may act as gate-keepers and how sessions can be made accessible and welcoming to fathers as well.*

- *Run some one-off events for fathers: this will be the starting point for your relationship-building and involvement work. Attendance at events for fathers is generally low; do not be discouraged if only very few join in. It will give you the opportunity to get to know some fathers better, and you may be able to find a keen father who can help you engage other men or who would be interested in volunteering in your setting. Use the events to discuss and plan further activities.*

- *Review your formal commitment to fathers: consider your prospectus and explore whether it may give hidden messages to mothers and fathers. Will both feel equally invited when they read it? You may want to add a clear statement on your commitment to working with fathers and detail the opportunities available to fathers in your setting. Your vision statement, parental involvement policy and other documents may need to be amended in the light of your changed practice to give clear messages about your commitment to working with fathers.*

C H A P T E R   S U M M A R Y

In this chapter you have looked at how you can engage with families who are not currently using your service and mothers and fathers who rarely come into your setting. Although we looked at several aspects of overcoming barriers to involvement in relation to different groups (hard-to-reach families, BME groups and fathers), the strategies discussed for each group are transferable and can effect positive change with a range of different families you may find difficult to engage in your setting. Two factors seem to be fundamental in effectively engaging with parents, firstly, the accessibility of the service and secondly, internal barriers. The services you offer should take the families as a starting point both figuratively and literally. This means offering more flexible services, for example including detached work at times which suit the families and in ways they find appropriate. It also means that your dialogue with them has to be based on the interests they identify and the problems they wish to address. At the same time you have to be mindful of how families may perceive you and your setting, including potentially negative past experiences and current cultural or religious considerations which may need to be sensitively addressed before parents can engage with you. You explored a range of different approaches and strategies to encourage families' involvement in your setting and considered action you can take within your setting to bring about change in the work with parents.

Self-assessment questions

1 Explain how data collection can support your work with BME families.

2 What are the main benefits and potential drawbacks of employing a staff member from a BME group to your Early Years team?

3 What are the main factors which facilitate a father's involvement in their children's learning?

Moving on

The following chapter will look at adult learning and provide the opportunity to consider how you can support mothers and fathers to understand their child's development better and how you can use volunteering for the benefit of the individual and of your setting. It will include ideas and strategies on working with your staff team to help them develop and to effect the changes in practice you would like to introduce. How you can prevent or overcome problems in your relationships with parents once they are involved in your setting will be explored in Chapter 7, while Chapter 8 will provide a more in-depth look at working with the community outside your setting.

Arnold, C (2007) Persistence pays off: working with parents who find our services 'hard to reach', in Whalley, M and the Pen Green Centre Team (ed) *Involving parents in their children's learning.* London: Paul Chapman Publishing, pp33–50.

ATD Fourth World (2006) *Not too hard to reach – developing a tool to reach the most disadvantaged families.* London: ATD Fourth World.

Burgess, A (2008) *Engaging fathers in their children's learning: tips for practitioners.* (Downloaded from **www.fatherhoodinstitute.org.index.php?id=12&c&D=323** on 8th November 2008)

Coe, C, Gibson, A, Spencer, N, and Stuttaford, M (2008) Sure Start: voices of the 'hard-to-reach'. *Child: care, health and development*, 34(4): 447–453.

Craig, G (2007) The elephant on the sofa: Sure Start and black and minority ethnic populations, in Anning, A and Ball, M (eds) *Improving services for young children, from Sure Start to children's centres.* London: SAGE Publications Ltd. pp48–61.

Department for Education and Skills (2004) *Engaging fathers – involving parents, raising achievements.* Nottingham: DfES Publications.

Desforges, C and Abouchaar, A (2003) *The impact of parental involvement, parental support and family education on pupil achievements and adjustment: a literature review* (Research Report 443), Nottingham: DfES Publications.

Kahn, T (2005) *Fathers involvement in Early Years settings, findings from research: (Executive Summary).* Pre-school Learning Alliance. (Downloaded from **www.pre-school.org/research/** on 18 November 2008).

Kahn, T (2006) *Involving fathers in Early Years Settings: evaluating four models for effective practice development (executive summary).* Pre-school Learning Alliance. (Downloaded from **www.pre-school.org/research/** on 18th November 2008).

Lloyd, N and Rafferty, A (2006) *Black and minority ethnic families and Sure Start: findings from local evaluation reports.* (Downloaded from **www.ness.bbk.ac.uk/documents/synthesisReports/1289.pdf** on 12th November 2008).

National Evaluation of Sure Start (NESS) (2003) *Fathers in Sure Start.* (Downloaded from **www.surestart.gov.uk/_doc/P0001408.pdf** on 10th November 2008).

Pascal, C and Bertram, T (2004) Sure Start: for everyone, inclusion pilot projects summary report, DfES, May, quoted in Lloyd, N and Rafferty, A (2006) *Black and minority ethnic families and Sure Start: findings from local evaluation reports.* (Downloaded from **www.ness.bbk.ac.uk/documents/synthesisReports/1289.pdf** on 12th November 2008).

Quinton, D (2004) *Supporting parents: messages from research.* London and Philadelphia: Jessica Kingsley Publisher.

Sheppard, M, MacDonald, P and Welbourne, P (2008) Service users as gatekeepers in children's centres. *Child and Family Social Work*, 13: 61–71.

Sylva (1999), in Arnold, C (2007) *Persistence pays off: working with parents who find our services 'hard to reach'.* Whalley, M and Chandler, T (2007), Parents and staff as co-educators – parents' means fathers too, in Whalley, M and the Pen Green Centre Team (ed), *Involving parents in their children's learning.* London: Paul Chapman Publishing, pp66–85.

FURTHER READING

Arnold, C (2007) Persistence pays off: working with parents who find our services 'hard to reach', in Whalley, M and the Pen Green Centre Team (ed) *Involving parents in their children's learning.* London: Paul Chapman Publishing, pp33–50.
Read for practical ideas of how to overcome barriers to parental involvement in their children's education and learning.

Craig, G and Adamson, S, Ali, N, Ali, S, Dadze-Arthur, A, Elliot, C, McNamee, S and Murtuja, B (2007) *National evaluation summary Sure Start and black minority ethnic populations.* Nottingham: DfES Publications.
Useful information on effective approaches to the work with BME groups.

Save the Children (2007) *Early Years outreach practice – supporting early years practitioners working with Gypsy, Roma and Traveller families*. Leeds: Save the Children.
Contains practical suggestions for Early Years work with Traveller families including many examples of successful projects.

USEFUL WEBSITES

www.childrens-centres.org

www.ormiston.org
Information and resources for the work with Travellers and fathers.

www.fatherhoodinstitute.org
Information and advice on working with fathers.

www.homeoffice.gov.uk/rds/pdfs2/dpr15.pdf
Research report on working with hard-to-reach families

6   The learning partnership

CHAPTER OBJECTIVES

After reading this chapter you should be able to:
- analyse the characteristics and needs of adult learners;
- identify effective adult learning experiences and processes;
- assess critically the learning opportunities you provide for adults in your setting;
- evaluate opportunities for adults and children to learn together.

This chapter develops your knowledge and understanding of how children, parents and professionals learn in your setting. The content is particularly relevant to 'S3', 'S29', 'S30', 'S31', 'S32' and 'S38' because these standards require you to reflect on how you work with parents to enhance their learning and that of their children. By gaining an understanding of how adults learn, you will be able to develop strategies to enhance parents' skills to support their children's learning, well-being, and development. At the same time you will reflect on your role as a learner in the context of your work setting and in relation to your colleagues. The learning from this chapter extends your expertise in the area of supporting transitions in the Common Core of Skills and Knowledge of the Children's Workforce.

Introduction

In the Early Years sector expectations for practice and quality are outlined by the Early Years Foundation Stage. Although not everybody agrees with the details of this framework, its emphasis on play in children's learning is widely supported. Children need to explore first hand, try out and test ideas, and learn through their senses while also being allowed the time and the opportunity to follow their own journeys of discovery. It is the role of the Early Years practitioner to facilitate their learning by providing stimulating environments, exciting opportunities and appropriate challenges which meet the developmental stages and needs of each individual child. You encourage young children to choose their own activities, interact and co-operate with their peers, and grow in independence.

If we look at a later stage in a child's life, for example to the start of secondary school at the age of 11 years, we find a more formal learning environment. Much of the school day is taken up with the transfer of knowledge from teacher to student in whole group situations rather than with experiential learning. The contents of lessons is often limited to what is expected for the next tests or examinations and most activities are teacher-led either by direct instruction or by completing practical tasks with clear guidance of what is to be done and how. Pupils have only limited opportunities to follow their own interests or direct their own learning. There is a strong emphasis on grades and achieving national targets and in spite of teachers and pupils agreeing learning targets for the term or year, these are set within the framework of the national curriculum. This is the type of learning environment many adults remember from their own schooling and although many would expect a learning environment for adults to be similar, we will need to explore whether this context creates the most effective approach to meeting adult learners' needs.

The main focus of your work will be the children and your desire to support their learning, but you have already explored in previous chapters how important the contributions from parents are in the development of their children. You have also touched on parenting courses and developing parenting skills as a way to enhance parents' support for their children but so far we have not considered the adult as a learner in detail. Adult learning styles, their motivation and their needs make many demands of the learning environment but within Early Years settings there is much scope to offer formal and informal learning opportunities for adults as well as children. Adult learning in Early Years settings has two different components, namely the parent as a learner and the Early Years practitioner as a learner. Their basic needs as adults who want to develop and progress professionally or personally are very similar but their respective roles mean that there are differences in their approach to the learning experience.

Adults as learners

In recent years there has been much emphasis on life-long learning and ongoing professional development in an attempt to ensure that the nation's workforce is better trained and has the capacity to keep the economy competitive in a large international

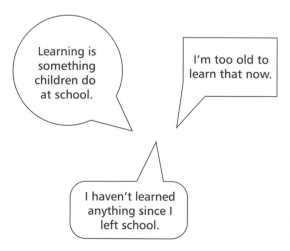

Figure 6.1 Comments on adults' capacity to learn

market. Although some adults feel learning is not for them, research evidence shows that adults have the potential to continue their cognitive development throughout their lives. Adulthood is not a stable phase in life but one which allows for and, more importantly, requires change and progression (Allman, 1983).

> *Up to the early part of the twentieth century the time-span of major cultural change (e.g. massive inputs of new knowledge, technological innovation, vocational displacement, population mobility, change in political and economic systems etc.) required several generations, whereas in the twentieth century several cultural revolutions have already occurred and the pace is accelerating. Under this new condition, knowledge is gained by the time a person is 21 and is largely obsolete by the time he is 40; and skills that made him productive in this twenties are becoming out of date during his thirties.*
>
> (Knowles, 1970, p55)

This pace of change is not slowing at the start of the twenty-first century and the need for adults to continue learning is ever-increasing. This is true for Early Years practitioners as well as mothers and fathers. There has been considerable change in the Early Years and childcare sector and parents find very different opportunities for their children and themselves than their own parents would have encountered. For Early Years Professionals the introduction of the Early Years Foundation Stage demands further learning and development so that this framework can be successfully incorporated into daily practice.

Earlier in this chapter we briefly sketched children's learning and the need to offer them the opportunity to learn through first-hand experience. Some adults prefer to learn by doing, while others favour more reflective ways of gaining new knowledge. These different approaches have been conceptualised by Honey and Mumford (1982) into four learning styles: activist, reflector, theorist and pragmatist.

> *Activists are people who learn by doing. They like to involve themselves in new experiences, and will 'try anything once'. They tend to act first and consider the consequences afterwards.*

Activists learn best when:

- *involved in new experiences, problems and opportunities;*
- *thrown in at the deep end;*
- *working with others in problem-solving, games, role-playing exercises;*
- *able to lead a group.*

Reflectors learn by observing and thinking about what happened. They like to consider all the possible angles and implications before coming to a considered opinion. They spend time listening and observing, and tend to be cautious and thoughtful.

Reflectors learn best when:

- *able to stand back and observe first;*
- *given time to think and investigate before commenting or acting;*

- *given an opportunity to review what has happened;*

- *doing tasks without tight deadlines.*

Theorists like to understand the theory behind the actions. They need models, concepts and facts in order to learn. They like to analyse and synthesise, and feel uncomfortable with subjective judgements.

Theorists learn best when:

- *an activity is backed up by ideas and concepts that form a model, system or theory;*

- *in a structured situation with a clear purpose;*

- *they have the chance to question and probe;*

- *required to understand a complex situation.*

Pragmatists are keen on trying things out. They look for ideas that can be applied to the problem in hand. They like to get on with things and tend to be impatient with open-ended discussions; they are practical, down-to-earth people.

Pragmatists learn best when:

- *there is an obvious link between the topic and a current need;*

- *they are shown techniques with clear practical advantage;*

- *they can try things out with feedback from an expert;*

- *they can copy an example, or emulate a role model.*

(Rosewell, 2004, pp1–4)

REFLECTIVE TASK

Think about yourself and your current learning experiences, be it to gain the Early Years Professional Status or during other studies. What type of learner are you? What about your colleagues? Do you think they have the same learning style? What does this mean for your work together?

FEEDBACK

You may feel that two rather than one learning style describe you best. Depending on circumstances or subject matter your preference may change slightly or you may favour a different combination. However, most people will lean towards a specific style and find the others more difficult to accommodate. This can have an impact on how well colleagues work together in a team. If you are the only person in your team who is, for example, an activist while everybody else are reflectors or theorists, you can easily feel isolated or continuously misunderstood. If everybody in the team favours the same learning style, it makes meetings, training sessions and joint working easy because everybody will agree, for example, to spend several meetings exploring all the issues, considering various options and gradually moving towards a decision. On the other hand, it could also make a team stagnant because there is little mutual challenge. The team is less likely to be able to draw strong connections between theory and practice if everybody favours a theoretical learning style. There is a danger that in situations where there is a need to act quickly, a team of reflectors will spend too much time deliberating and therefore miss valuable opportunities. When teams have a good mix of learning styles they can be very dynamic and vibrant with high levels of learning as theorists encourage pragmatists to embed their practice in principles and theories, reflectors help activists to review their actions, and pragmatists ensure that progress for the team and the work as a whole is not delayed by prolonged discussions. However, to achieve this, teams and individuals need to be aware and respectful of their individual differences and much will depend on you as the leader of your team to utilise positively the energy which flows in a mixed team and to limit the friction which could arise.

Young children learn through first-hand experience which develops their cognitive structures and these, in turn, shape their actions and behaviours. Regardless of their preferred learning styles, adults' learning follows the same pattern. A direct experience, which can be an incident in the nursery or an interesting journal article, influences their thinking which then has an impact on their behaviour or action (Easen *et al*, 1992). However, adults vary from children in a number of ways: their self-concept is more highly developed; they bring much more life experience; their motivation for learning is different; and they have a clearer focus for their learning (adapted from Knowles, 1970).

Self-concept

At birth babies are utterly dependent on the adults around them to meet all their needs and toddlers do not understand themselves as independent beings but experience their identity through external sources like their parents and siblings. From this self-concept based on dependency, children develop over time to become more independent. In adulthood the self-concept is based on being in control and self-directing, being able to make your own decisions and managing your life. This view of being independent, and the desire to maintain it, can lead to problems for adults in relation to learning situations. For many adults learning is associated with childhood and the teacher–learner relationship is understood to be based on dependency. Hence, adults may shrink from putting themselves into a learning situation but prefer to be doers or producers; they try to avoid contexts where they think they may be 'told what to do' to maintain their view of themselves as being self-directing and in control (also see the feedback on the following reflective task).

Experience

With increase in age adults gather an ever-growing amount of experience and are likely to have had many different, sometimes challenging, conflicting, exhilarating or life-changing, experiences. Adults identify themselves strongly through their history, where they have lived, what they have done, where they travelled to, which work they have done, and so on. Because of their varied experience, they will bring different backgrounds, life stories, and personalities to the learning situation which needs to acknowledge and value this experience, otherwise individuals may feel their identity and their personality are being ignored. This wealth of experience offers the adult a rich resource for his learning: he can, for example, compare and reflect on previous events; he can find solutions to his current problems by remembering how he overcame similar situations in the past; he can link theory to the practice in his own life. The experience of an adult is, in addition, not just a resource for his own learning but can significantly enrich the learning of others. In group situations the combined experience of the adults can help individual participants to reflect on and find solutions to problems in their own lives.

Motivation

From research and experience we know that children's development can be conceptualised by different stages often including sequential milestones. Throughout their development particular periods or time windows appear when they are ready to learn certain skills. During these teachable moments learning is highly effective while it is impossible or difficult at earlier or later points in time. Although adults no longer progress through fixed stages or milestones in their lives, there are phases when they want to learn new skills or gain new understanding. These phases are normally linked to social changes like starting a new job, moving house, or having a baby. Their child starting at pre-school or nursery can also be a phase when adults feel their role is changing and they are keen to learn about their child at this different stage of development or about the nursery she is going to and how they can get involved. These transition stages present good windows of opportunity for you to engage with mothers and fathers and encourage their learning.

Learning focus

In our schools much of the learning for children is divided into subject areas. However, when adults recognise the need to learn and develop their understanding or skills, this is normally linked to a specific problem they want to address. A problem-based approach to learning is therefore likely to be more suitable than a subject-based one. In addition, the learning context should offer adults the opportunity to apply new learning in practice so that they can almost immediately start addressing the problems in their daily lives which have given rise to their need to learn.

These four factors indicate that adults are very different to children in their approach to learning. At the same time individual learning styles need to be understood and respected so that adults can learn effectively. This has implications for the learning environment and learning situations you create for adults in your setting.

The adult learning experience

From the daily work in your Early Years setting you are used to organising the learning environment for young children and similar factors need to be considered for adults, but in the light of their particular needs the arrangements you make will be quite different. The physical environment is important, for example the layout of the room and the equipment or materials on offer, but so are the allocation of staff members, the aims and objectives for particular activities and the general ethos and principles your setting bases all its work on. In previous chapters we have mentioned many factors which support your involvement and partnership working with mothers and fathers, many of which are relevant to the learning context as well:

- arrange learning activities so that the timing suits parents with busy lives;

- ensure that the venue is suitable and easily accessible;

- offer crèche facilities so that young children are cared for while parents learn;

- be non-judgemental and anti-discriminatory in your practice;

- respect parents and acknowledge their competence;

- provide information in an appropriate and accessible format;

- consult to make sure the learning event you offer meets parents' needs;

- base your involvement with parents on the principles of a partnership of equals.

Each one of these factors seems to be linked to at least one of two aspects, either the environment (physical space, timing, availability of crèche) or the interactions of both parents and Early Years practitioners in and with this environment. These two aspects together add up to the basic unit of learning:

Environment + interaction = learning experience

Importantly, it is the teacher or, in your setting, the Early Years Professional who shapes both elements of this equation (Knowles, 1970). The environment you present to the learner and the interactions you initiate and encourage are crucial to the adult learning experience. Apart from the physical environment of appropriate seating, heating, suitable course material and so on, the atmosphere you create is very important. Adults appreciate a context which is friendly and informal where they are accepted, respected and supported. A formal set-up which stresses the difference in status between learner and teacher will not encourage adults to feel comfortable and engage successfully with the learning process. There is a danger that a more formal environment will give a sense of anonymity where adults are not personally known to the teacher and will therefore feel overlooked or ignored as individuals with their particular life experiences and circumstances.

In Chapter 4 you have already considered some features of an effective parenting course with a focus on the course materials and the overall framework. In addition, learning experiences that draw on active participation and value life experience are generally more effective, especially if there is an immediate opportunity to apply the new learning in day-to-day life. Because adults have very individual needs and specific reasons for learning they progress best if the learning programme develops out of a joint diagnosis of their needs, leading to objectives agreed together by learner and teacher. Adult learners are not overly concerned about grades as the learning itself is the more important aspect for them. A self-evaluation at the end of a workshop or period of learning is often more productive and it helps adults to reflect on their own progress, to judge whether objectives have been achieved and to plan further learning targets if need be or desired.

CASE STUDY

After regularly using the crèche for their children so that they can attend meetings and workshops in the children's centre some parents expressed an interest in volunteering as crèche workers. To support their development and prepare them for this work, the centre organised a 10-week course which was based on an Open College Network unit exploring the importance of play for young children. The crèche supervisor added some sessions focussing on the practical work in the crèche so that students would be familiar with routines and gained a wider insight into the crèche provision. A few weeks into the course it became clear that some of the participants were attending the course not just because they were interested in the crèche but because they were considering working with children as a future career. To help parents explore which type of childcare setting they may want to consider as a workplace, the crèche supervisor helped some interested parents to arrange short-term placements in the day nursery attached to the children's centre, in a nursery class at the local primary school, and in a pre-school. Participants shared their experiences with the whole group which enabled those who had not taken part in the placements to gain an insight into the different type of childcare provision as well. With the help of local authority staff it was possible to add further career guidance sessions which helped participants to explore which age ranges and types of settings they may want to work in.

This flexible approach to the contents and length of the course meant that all of the 13 participants who started also finished the course and gained their Open College Network credits. Three of the learners started to volunteer regularly in the children's centre crèche provision, two became volunteers in the day nursery and enrolled for NVQ Level 2 training, one parent decided that she wanted to work in a school setting and explored further training to help her become a teaching assistant. Two parents regularly use their new knowledge and understanding to support faith-based family activity groups.

FEEDBACK

When offering courses which lead to specific credits or awards it is not always possible to change the contents but there is normally an opportunity to extend the programme to address particular areas of interest suggested by the learners. This allows for a combination of and compromise between what the course prescribes and what the students want to learn. Responding to the learners' needs does not necessarily mean you have to tailor a whole course to their wishes but that you are open-minded and flexible. Through discussion and negotiation with the learner you can find the balance between individual learning needs and the requirements of a specific credit or award.

REFLECTIVE TASK

How would you assess the learning experience during your current course to gain Early Years Professional Status (or during other studies)? Does it value your life experience? Do you think it meets your learning needs?

FEEDBACK

Many adults remember their own time at school as a period of frustration: they were told what to do, they had little independence, and they were not able to follow their own interests. As mentioned earlier, negative experiences can act as a barrier to adults engaging in new learning. In spite of unhappy learning experiences as children, adults are not necessarily prepared for or keen on engaging in more independent or self-directed ways of learning where they have to take responsibility for their own development. Although they do not like it, they still expect the traditional approach where the teacher teaches and the learner passively listens and learns. When the teaching approach is different, their initial reaction may be one of anger, frustration and confusion. Adult teachers have to support their learners through a period of adjustment to help them accept and adopt new ways of learning so that learning becomes the responsibility of both the teacher and the learner with the learner playing a very active part and the teacher supporting rather than leading this process.

> *Andragogy (the art and science of helping adults learn) assumes that a teacher can't really 'teach' in the sense of 'make a person learn', but that one person can only help another person learn.*

(Knowles, 1970, p60)

This may reflect your own experience or that of some of your colleagues on your course. You may also encounter the expectation of traditional approaches to learning when trying to work with parents in your setting. If you respond to their requests to be 'taught' it is likely that they become despondent and resentful very quickly as this traditional approach is in conflict with their self-concept as adults (see above) and does not help them to have their needs as learners met appropriately.

We established that both environment and interaction add up to the learning experience and we have explored this equation in the more traditional context of the classroom setting where teachers and learners get together specifically to learn. However, as adults learn better in less formal environments and are motivated to learn by needs within their daily lives, it seems worth exploring whether learning can become part of these daily lives rather than being seen as a separate activity. Many parents enjoy the relaxed atmosphere and social interaction in toddler groups, children's centre play sessions or drop-in coffee mornings, and make them part of their family's weekly routines. These sessions have the potential for adult learning which in some of them may already be utilised, for example by a visitor coming into the group giving a short talk, or by staff members being available for question and answer style sessions with a particular topic. The group leader or a parent may stimulate a discussion during which adults can learn from each others' experience. Home-visits, progress reviews and volunteering tasks can also present opportunities for adult learning. Seen as individual events these activities seem to present a rather fragmented approach to learning. However, if there is thorough planning with a clear vision regarding the intended learning outcomes and a structured approach to the delivery of all the various opportunities, then individual sessions can build on each other to re-inforce and extend learning. This is akin to extending a child's understanding of the concept of 'more than' at the playdough table, in the sand pit and during the cooking activity over a period of many days in a pre-school setting.

CASE STUDY

After several parents from the Rainbow Toddler Group had been talking about their children falling and hurting themselves the leader arranged for a visit from the St John's Ambulance Service. At the next session this visitor talked to parents about how they could handle minor cuts and bruises effectively either at home or while they are out and about. Families really appreciated the opportunity to ask lots of questions and the group decided to invite somebody from the ambulance service to come once a month to talk about different aspects of first aid.

FEEDBACK

In the informal atmosphere of the toddler group adults who may not think of themselves as learners and would shrink from a traditional course or classroom environment can find it easy to engage in learning.

Volunteering can offer adults many learning opportunities, for example by developing book-keeping skills as the treasurer for the pre-school committee, extending their understanding of children's play when helping in the classroom, or practising their organisational skills while planning and running the Christmas fayre. To enable adults to learn effectively while volunteering, there needs to be adequate support in place.

REFLECTIVE TASK

Consider how you could help volunteers in your setting to develop their knowledge and skills and what support they may need.

Volunteering is most successful when both the volunteer and the setting benefit from the co-operation. It is important to gain some clarity on:

- *what the volunteer would like to do;*

- *what he or she is trying to gain from volunteering;*

- *what skills he or she brings to the role;*

- *whether new knowledge and skills are required;*

- *what the setting would like to gain;*

- *what training and support it can offer;*

- *who will be responsible for the volunteer and his or her work;*

- *practical matters like when and where the volunteering activity is taking place.*

To help both parties it may be useful to draw up a 'volunteer agreement' covering the above points and a 'task description' which outlines the activities of the volunteer and the objectives he is trying to achieve. The latter can help the volunteer to take responsibility for his own learning by specifying what he wants to achieve. You or other staff members can provide support by providing appropriate induction activities, overseeing the work, and offering supervisions. In supervisions you can clarify work issues with the volunteer but also help him to reflect on his volunteering experience and the related learning and to plan next steps (also see Chapter 7).

Developing parenting skills

Regardless of whether you are placing learning in the classroom or in the informal environment of a drop-in session, in a supervision meeting or a volunteering activity, the actual teaching methods (in the sense of helping somebody to learn) you employ will to some extent depend on what adults want to learn. If you want to learn how to bandage a badly cut knee (a physical skill), a demonstration followed by a hands-on attempt are likely to be helpful. This is learning in the psychomotor domain; you need some knowledge but the emphasis is on physical dexterity and practice. If you want to know how you can integrate the Early Years Foundation Stage into the practice in your setting, you need to learn in the cognitive domain. The methods to use are those which stimulate thinking, like discussions, case studies, tutorials, buzz groups, and workshops. The third learning domain is the affective one which addresses our attitudes, feelings and emotions, for example our assumptions and views of a Black Minority Ethnic group. Learning in the affective domain is best supported by discussions and debates, role play and one-to-one sessions (Reece and Walker, 1997). Consequently, if you want to support mothers and fathers in their role as parents, you need to clarify first what it is they want to learn. There are many different skills which are summarised as 'parenting skills' and parents may want to know more about how to help their children when they fall and hurt themselves (psychomotor domain), or they may want to know how their children's thinking develops (cognitive domain). The nature of these topics suggests different teaching strategies and different learning environments. The former can be addressed with a first aid course run by a qualified trainer from the British Red Cross, the latter with a workshop on brain development in babies and toddlers. Alternatively, parents can learn what they want to know during a practical demonstration in a drop-in or by volunteering in the classroom where they can observe different children and their interactions with Early Years practitioners; both formal and informal teaching methods would be suitable.

REFLECTIVE TASK

Consider which role you play in the formal and informal learning experiences for parents in your setting. Is this a role you are aware of and actively develop and plan for?

FEEDBACK

For a first aid course you are likely to engage a qualified trainer and your role is that of the facilitator or organiser rather than the teacher but in many other cases you are the expert in the field and hence are likely be the best person to help parents gain new knowledge and understanding, for example when parents have questions about their children's behaviour or lack of progress. Apart from this more overt role, there is an informal, often overlooked teaching role for Early Years practitioners. In most settings parents observe practitioners consciously or unconsciously every time they come into the nursery room or activity session. Staff members therefore always model appropriate behaviour and parents will learn through observation. Similarly, when parents ask for advice on parenting issues, Early Years practitioners can use their response to create valuable learning opportunities by working more closely with this family to gain the skills or understanding they need to overcome their problem. Your own role will include both working directly with the parents and enabling your team members to be aware of and utilise learning opportunities in the daily life of your setting. As in your work with the children in your setting, the unplanned experiences can often be the most rewarding ones but staff members need to be able to recognise them and feel confident to utilise them to maximum effect.

In addition to the more practical aspects mentioned, 'parenting skills' also include how mothers and fathers interact with their children, how they understand their own role in relation to their child, and how they respond emotionally to their children's behaviour. These skills are shaped by parents' self-concept, their own life and particularly childhood experiences, and their attitudes and feelings about children and their behaviour. In addition, real or perceived cultural expectations influence strongly how parents behave towards and respond to their children. To enhance parenting skills is therefore not simply a question of teaching a practical skill (like how to change a nappy) or explaining developmental stages but also a question of how you can support parents to explore their attitudes and to try and change them.

Louise has been involved in the Parents' Involvement in Their Children's Learning (PICL) group at the Pen Green Centre in Corby. She says:

> *When I first went to the group, it was just brilliant knowing why he was doing things, especially the throwing, because he used to throw everything, and obviously that was his trajectory schema. They told me that he was going on to learn about areas and everything to do with mathematics and things, and I was thinking, 'Wow', and it took a little while to sink in, really. But then, as I went to the group, I learnt more and more why he was doing things at nursery, and it was relatively easy to see what he was doing at home. Sean used to flood my bathroom; he liked to see the water overflowing. Before, I was getting really angry because it was, like, so-called naughty things he was doing. Obviously, it still is a bit naughty sometimes, because you don't want your bathroom soaked or whatever, but why he was doing it was because he was learning. I used to try and think of alternative things for him to do which wasn't wrecking my house and being dangerous.*

> (Cummings, 2007, p110)

Initially Louise saw her son's behaviour as naughty but by learning about schemas she was able to develop a different way of explaining what he was doing. She now does not get angry with him but tries to find alternative activities for him to enhance his learning. The way she is parenting Sean has changed considerably; not getting angry with him will support a more positive relationship between them and she is influencing his learning by offering him valuable alternatives to less desirable activities.

Mezirow (1981) describes this change in the way we see things as a 'perspective trans-formation' and understands it as an emancipatory process as it allows us to become aware of and overcome the structures and assumptions which constrain our thinking. To stay with Louise and Sean as an example, Louise faced the problem of Sean's difficult and naughty behaviour. She was able to share this with others in the PICL group where she explored new ways of explaining his behaviour (using schemas) and then she gradually developed her own understanding of them. This led to her changing her response to Sean's throwing and playing with water. Other people may still describe his behaviour as naughty but with her newly gained understanding and her alternative response to Sean's play and learning, she has overcome the social constraints which expect her to stop his behaviour. She has the understanding now to explain his behaviour and to work with it to progress Sean's learning and development.

Supporting adult learners to go through such a perspective transformation demands more of the teacher than passing on information or demonstrating a motor skill. The teacher should arrange for learning experiences which challenge taken-for-granted assumptions and attitudes, help parents to examine different options to find solutions to their problems, develop their confidence, and support them to try out new approaches and responses (Mezirow, 1981). As an Early Years Professional you may not necessarily see this support for parents' learning as your primary role or your field of expertise, but the potential impact of enhanced parenting skills on children is considerable and their learning, development and well-being will increase substantially. Furthermore, while you are engaged in supporting the parent's learning you have the opportunity to learn more about the parent as well. This will contribute to the learning partnership in which children, parents and professionals learn together (see below).

Early Years practitioners as learners

Although we have considered adult learning in relation to parents in your setting, the same principles and approaches apply to the other adults in your setting, the staff members.

REFLECTIVE TASK

Through your studies to gain an Early Years qualification you are likely to be deeply involved in learning at the moment. How much of this takes place in your work place? Are you learning from your colleagues? From the parents and children?

FEEDBACK

Learning in the workplace takes many forms, it can be self-initiated, part of your routine, or stimulated by others. You may try out activities and approaches you heard about on your course to see how they translate into your practice; through observing children at play you can deepen your understanding of particular aspects of child development. In dialogue with colleagues your thinking about a developmental theory may get challenged and you reassess its value for your work; in a team meeting a colleague cascades information and insights from a recent training event; a parent brings in books and objects to explain a religious festival; in your professional journal you reflect on a critical incident at work and your emotional response to it.

There are countless learning opportunities for staff members in an Early Years setting, and part of your role as an Early Years Professional is to help colleagues use these and progress their own development. As with other adult learners you may want to agree learning objectives either with individual team members in their supervision meetings or with the whole team to enhance the overall practice in your setting. The learning needs will be linked to all three domains (psychomotor, cognitive and affective) and will often be interrelated. The challenge for many team leaders, lead professionals and managers is to change staff members' attitudes and assumptions, for example their opinions on teenage parents or their reservations regarding partnership working with parents. Mezirow's dynamics for the process of perspective transformation may be a useful tool to guide you through the stages of change in your colleagues' thinking (see Table 6.1).

Table 6.1   Dynamics of perspective transformation

	Dynamics of perspective transformation	Practical example
1	A disorienting dilemma.	A girl from the Travellers' community is not progressing towards expected milestones.
2	Self-examination.	Encourage the team member to ask herself: am I supporting her sufficiently? How much time do I spend with her? Do I enjoy being with her?
3	A critical assessment of personally internalized role assumptions and a sense of alienation from traditional social expectations.	Support the team member to assess: what do I know about Travellers? Are these facts or assumptions which may influence how I talk to her and what I expect of her? Why should this little girl not achieve as well as others?
4	Relating one's discontent to similar experiences of others or to public issues – recognizing that one's problem is shared and not exclusively a private matter.	Facilitate sharing of the dilemma and thoughts in team meetings to explore whether others are having similar problems in their groups; exploring wider issues relating to the Travellers' community.
5	Exploring options for new ways of acting.	Stimulate discussions with colleagues in the setting, with professionals from other organisations working with the Travellers' community, and with the parents of the girl.
6	Building competence and self-confidence in new roles.	Support the colleague to gain new skills and insight, maybe by visiting a Travellers' site to develop contacts with families and overcoming geographical and emotional barriers. Observe the colleague and give positive feedback; enhance self-confidence.
7	Planning a course of action.	Guide the team members (and maybe the whole team) towards agreeing a structured plan for change.
8	Acquiring knowledge and skills for implementing one's plans.	Facilitate consultation with, for example, the Travellers' Education Service and discuss planned action.
9	Provisional efforts to try new roles and to assess feedback.	Give constructive and frequent feedback, review sessions with the team member and parents to ensure that the team member feels comfortable in her new role and that there is change in the development of the young girl..
10	A reintegration into society on the basis of conditions dictated by the new perspective.	Support the team member in her new way of working and acting when she is challenged by colleagues or the wider community.

(Adapted from Mezirow, 1981, p127)

A transformation of people's thinking does not always come as one sudden insight but can be characterised by a series of transitions. Your role includes drawing the link between separate transitions and clarifying the direction of change. You obviously also have a much wider role in arranging learning and development opportunities to support the team of practitioners in your setting. We briefly discuss leading learning at the end of this chapter but you will find more information and a fuller discussion in the book *Leading Practice in Early Years Setting* by M.E Whalley *et al* in this series.

Parents, children and professionals learning together

Parents and professionals are both adult learners and share the same needs regarding the learning experience; they face similar facilitating or inhibiting factors and may all find some learning situations productive, challenging, or unsatisfying. As discussed above, a key element in the adult learning experience is the interaction between the learner and his environment. This environment is not limited to physical aspects like the room where the learning takes place, the materials used or the resources available. One key aspect of the learning environment are the people involved in it, the learner with his life experience which can support his own and the learning of others, and the teacher with his life experience and professional knowledge. The interaction or dialogue between the learners, and between the learners and their teacher offers rich learning opportunities.

CASE STUDY

During the story time session with the children's librarian Hannah complained that her son Ben wanted her to read the same book over and over again and it did not seem worth while borrowing any other books – Ben would just not want to look at them. The librarian spent some time with Hannah explaining how children's language develops through constant repetition and that Ben was in the process of understanding the story and learning the words linked to it. She encouraged Hannah to observe closely what Ben was doing while she was reading. At the beginning of the next story time session Hannah reported that Ben paid very close attention while she was reading but did not say much. However, she had noticed when he was playing with his older brother he had tried to use some of the words from the story, and although his pronunciation was not perfect, he used the words in the right context. The librarian chose some stories for her session which included the words Ben had used so that he could hear them again and extend his understanding of their meaning.

In the children's centre, two staff members run a play and learning course. Each session starts with the parents and staff on their own for an hour while the children are cared for in a crèche. They explore different development areas and stages and discuss how parents can support their children's play. During the second hour the parents join the children in the crèche room and have the opportunity to engage with their children in play activities linked to their earlier theory session. Staff members support parents to put their new learning into practice but also step back to observe how parents and children engage with each other. They discuss their observations with individual parents and explore some play ideas for the family to try at home. The feedback from the home play then provides the starting point for the next session.

FEEDBACK

In both case studies, adults and children learn together either in an informal way, or in the more formal setting of a short course. When parents and Early Years practitioner share their observations of children and plan their play together they complement each other with the professional contributing the general theory about child development and the parent bringing a personal theory about the development of her particular child (see Easen et al 1992). Both adults are learners in this context: the Early Years practitioner learns more about an individual child and his development and deepens her understanding of the theory through application in practice. She can learn more about how parents perceive and understand their children and develop more sensitive and effective ways of engaging them in their children's learning. If there is a co-worker then there is also scope to learn by observing different practice and by exploring his or her approaches and ideas. The parent learns about her own child and his development and about the underlying general theory. With the help of the professional she can explore her assumptions of her own role and her relationships with her child. This joint learning between adults leads to more effective and stimulating learning experiences for the child and all three benefit from the dialogue between adults by gaining new knowledge and understanding. As the child learns, his behaviour will change which will initiate further dialogue and interaction between 'his adults'. Parent, child and professional truly learn in partnership and stimulate the development of each others' understanding and knowledge.

Engaging the parent in his child's learning and development is likely to be the motivation for your work with parents but we have seen in earlier chapters that parents may find it difficult to participate in the activities you offer for them. As with initial engagement and relationship building, the starting point for the dialogue with parents about their children's learning needs to be the parent and their observations and interpretations of their child's behaviour. Not all parents will feel ready for the dialogue and you may need to address the parents' anxieties and issues first before they can focus on their child. This means that the parent and his or her learning have to become more central to your work. Through the learning experiences of the parent you can stimulate and enhance the home learning environment for the child and through your own learning in the dialogue with the parent you can make more suitable provision for the child's learning in your setting.

Leading learning

Your role as the Early Years Professional in the context of the learning partnership between professionals, parents and children is two-fold. On the one hand you are an active participant in the learning experiences and on the other you are the leader or facilitator of the whole learning ethos and environment in your setting. As a team leader you have the opportunity to encourage and support colleagues to engage in learning, either individually in supervisions or collectively in team meetings. Colleagues will also perceive you as a role model and will look to you as an example of a professional who embraces learning in her daily working life.

REFLECTIVE TASK

What do you think are the characteristics of a 'learning leader', a professional who learns herself and encourages others to learn?

FEEDBACK

It is not possible to sum up in just a few words what makes a good leader in general or a good leader of learning in particular. Here are just some characteristics which are relevant and start to describe some of the attributes of a learning leader:

- *curiosity (an interest in learning);*

- *honesty (principles and actions being open to public scrutiny and a willingness to speak the truth);*

- *courtesy (treating others with respect and dignity);*

- *courage (a willingness to risk and dare and a willingness to make mistakes and learn from them);*

- *compassion (creating trust, empathy, high expectations, hope and inspiration and providing opportunities for individual, group, personal and professional development).*
(Rodd, 2006, p37)

Embedding a learning ethos and extending the learning to include children, parents and professionals may require a change in your setting's culture. This will not be easy as it involves substantial learning in its own right and cannot be brought about by just one person. As an Early Years Professional you are, however, ideally placed to initiate the process and engage others in bringing about change in your setting. It is important, though, to remember that:

> *Learning and change cannot be imposed on people. Their involvement and participation is needed in diagnosing what is going on, in figuring out what to do, and in actually bringing about learning and change. The more turbulent, ambiguous, and out of control the world becomes, the more the learning process must be shared by all the members of the social unit doing the learning.*

(Schein, 2004, p418)

C H A P T E R   S U M M A R Y

In this chapter we developed the concept of the learning partnership in Early Years settings acknowledging the difference between children's learning and adult learning. Adult learning principles are based on the understanding that parents are self-directing, knowledgeable, and competent adults who should be encouraged to actively engage with and define their own learning needs according to individual circumstances. The underlying values and the corresponding approach to engaging parents in learning are therefore the same as those identified in earlier chapters for general parental involvement work. To engage parents effectively in their children's development, learning and well-being, Early Years practitioners must be aware of different adult learning styles and able to respond appropriately to parents' different learning needs. In addition to the parent as a learner you identified other professionals and yourself as learners within the partnership which also includes the children as each stimulates development and learning in the other. The role of the Early Years Professional is particularly important for the partnership as you are not just a learner yourself but also in a position to facilitate a learning ethos in your setting and encourage others to engage in the learning process.

Self-assessment questions

1 What are the key characteristics of adult learners?

2 What are the benefits and challenges of having staff members with different learning styles working together?

3 Explain the role of the Early Years Professional in relation to the learning partnership of parent, professional and child.

Moving on

To explore further how you can support parents to gain an understanding of child development concepts and how parents and professionals can learn together, look at the Pen Green Centre in Corby with their long tradition of partnership working to support children's learning and development. Details on wider family learning opportunities and courses are available through your Local Authority and you may be able to work in co-operation with them to enhance parents' basic skills and parenting skills.

REFERENCES

Allman, P (1983) The nature and process of adult development, in Tight, M (ed) *Adult learning and development*. Buckingham: Open University Press.

Cummings, A (2007) The impact on parents, in Whalley, M and the Pen Green Centre Team (ed) *Involving parents in their children's learning*. London: Paul Chapman Publishing, pp105–121.

Easen, P, Kendall, P and Shaw, J (1992), Parents and educators: dialogue and development through partnership. *Children and Society*, 6(4): 282–296.

Honey, P and Mumford, A (1982) *A manual of learning styles*. Maidenhead: Peter Money.

Knowles, M.S (1970), Andragogy: an emerging technology for adult learning, reprinted from Knowles, MS *The modern practice of adult education: from pedagogy to andragogy*, Cambridge: Cambridge Book Company.

Mezirow, J (1981) A critical theory of adult learning and education: *Adult Education*, 32(1).

Reece, I and Walker, S (1997) *Teaching, training and learning; a practical guide*, 3rd edition. Sunderland: Business Education Publishers Limited.

Rosewell, J (2004) *Learning styles*. Buckingham: The Open University. (Downloaded from **www.openlearn.open.ac.uk/file.php/1715/Learning%20styles.pdf** on 6 December 2008.)

Rodd, J (2006) *Leadership in early childhood*. Maidenhead: Open University Press.

Schein, EH (2004) *Organizational culture and leadership*. San Francisco: Jossey-Bass

FURTHER READING

Knowles, MS (1970) Andragogy: an emerging technology for adult learning, reprinted from Knowles, MS, *The modern practice of adult education: from pedagogy to andragogy*. Cambridge: Cambridge Book Company.
Gives an insight into adult learning and offers principles of adult teaching.

Whalley, ME and the Pen Green Centre Team (ed) *Involving parents in their children's learning*. London: Paul Chapman Publishing.
Describes how the staff team at the Pen Green Centre engage parents in their children's learning.

Whalley, ME, Allen, S and Wilson, D (2008) *Leading Practice in Early Years Settings*. Exeter: Learning Matters Publishing.
This book explores how you can effectively lead practice in your setting including how you can support colleagues to develop their confidence and how your team can work towards better outcomes for children.

USEFUL WEBSITES

www.familylearning.org.uk
Information and advice on parents and children learning together.

www.learndirect.co.uk
Offers adult learning opportunities.

www.volunteering.org.uk
Information on how to work with volunteers including useful draft agreements, policies and other necessary paperwork.

www.lsc.gov.uk
Learning and Skills Council Website.

www.niace.org.uk
National Institute of Adult Continuing Education

7 When partnerships get difficult

CHAPTER OBJECTIVES

After reading this chapter you should be able to:
- assess the need for transparency and confidentiality in Early Years settings;
- assess critically different approaches to reducing conflict and improving relationships with parents in difficult circumstances;
- analyse effective communication tools to maintain the dialogue with parents;
- analyse the role of monitoring and evaluation in an Early Years setting.

This chapter develops your knowledge and understanding of how you can effectively work with parents when your relationships with them are complex or strained. The content is particularly relevant to 'S30' and 'S31' because these standards require you to reflect on your approach to working in partnership and maintaining effective communication with parents to enhance their children's learning. Furthermore, the chapter relates to 'S33' and 'S38' as it explores how your setting's culture and ethos can support effective communication in difficult circumstances and to 'S20' as it considers relationships with parents when children are in danger or at risk of harm. The learning from this chapter is particularly relevant to the following areas of expertise outlined by the Common Core of Skills and Knowledge for the Children's Workforce: child and young person development, safeguarding and promoting the welfare of the child, multi-agency working and sharing information (DfES, 2005).

Introduction

You started your reflections on your work with parents by exploring your attitudes towards them and considering different issues relating to the initial engagement with them. This was followed by exploring how you can involve parents in their children's Early Years experiences and support the learning and development of both the children and the adults. In this context we mentioned the different roles for parents in an Early Years setting, for example as volunteers or as committee members. If parents assume additional roles and responsibilities beyond those of being a parent, your relationship with them will change, which in turn may give rise to problems and conflict. In this chapter you will reflect on some of the causes of difficulties in the relationships with individual parents due to their different roles and consider strategies which can help you avoid or overcome conflict situations. You will look at good working practices with parents as neighbours, friends and employers, and reflect on the practical aspect of maintaining effective communication when there are concerns about parenting skills and about the safety and well-being of children. Throughout this chapter you will draw on the learning from previous chapters regarding general principles of partnership working, parental involvement and adult learning.

When parents are employers, neighbours and friends

The parents you encounter in your work environment are not just parents; they are also neighbours, friends, volunteers, scout leaders, relatives, employers, and much more. In some cases they may be your neighbours, members of your family, your friends, leaders in your children's scout pack, or your employer. Neighbours relate differently to each other than employer and employee do, the way friends behave varies from the way family members interact, and so on. These different relationships, which can exist between the same two people depending on the situation they find themselves in, can lead to a confusion of roles and hence to uncertainty about what constitutes appropriate behaviour. If these different relationships and ensuing uncertainties are not acknowledged and discussed, they can lead to misunderstanding, disagreement and ultimately open conflict. Trying to avoid conflict is a normal human reaction, we deny its existence, ignore it, or belittle it. These are, however, behaviours developing out of a very negative view of conflict and are not necessarily helpful in resolving a conflict permanently. In your Early Years setting you will, for example, want to embrace diversity and acknowledge the different families and cultures the children come from and support the development of their emerging identities in the context of their communities. This means accepting and working with the differences children and their parents bring to your work. The conflict that arises out of different views may challenge long-established practice and assumptions and force you to review your practice but the outcomes of this conflict do not need to be negative. On the contrary, they can be positive as conflict urges us to reflect, learn and develop, to provide better care and education for the children, and to build more respectful relationships with parents.

In your reflections on working in partnership with parents you have already established approaches based on mutual trust and respect for others including valuing the contributions others make and accepting parents as equal partners. A collaborative and democratic ethos in your setting provides an effective framework for parental involvement and partnership working between parents and Early Years practitioners. At the same time it also creates an environment which is conducive to addressing the conflict which may arise out of your work with parents and their different roles in relation to you and your colleagues. Below you will explore some situations which could potentially lead to conflict and consider different approaches to overcoming these; although different strategies will be linked to particular situations it is likely that they will also be useful and effective tools in other circumstances.

Parents as volunteers

When parents volunteer to help in the nursery classroom or become a committee member, the professionals' relationship with this parent changes and the new roles and responsibilities need clarifying. How this can be done you have already considered in Chapter 6 but an additional question is how other parents will perceive this new relationship. Some may feel that the parent in question is given preferential treatment, that Early Years practitioners 'are getting their friends onto the committee' or that a parent is trying to gain favours.

REFLECTIVE TASK

How could you avoid these suspicious feelings arising amongst parents when one of them takes on an additional role in your setting?

FEEDBACK

If parents are clearer about how volunteers are selected they may feel less resentful. You may want to ensure that the offer to volunteer is made to all parents. An application process may be helpful, not just to avoid thoughts of favouritism but also to ensure that volunteers take on roles and responsibilities that are appropriate to their interests, skills and capacity. If it is likely that there will be too many requests for volunteering, a panel of staff, parents, and committee representatives considering applications may bring objectivity to the selection process.

Committee or partnership board members should be elected by the parents themselves. A parent forum may provide a good venue for parent candidates to introduce themselves; drop-ins, newsletters, or the nursery website may also allow candidates to canvass and encourage as many parents as possible to take part in the vote.

Processes that are transparent and easy to understand will avoid many difficulties arising from the selection of volunteers and committee members. Being clear about what the expectations are and what their roles and responsibilities entail will also prevent disagreements with the volunteers themselves. Some of your policies and procedures will relate to how volunteers, staff members, and committee members work together but special attention should be paid to how this is communicated. Good induction processes give the opportunity to discuss different roles and expectations and clarify areas of uncertainty. Regularly evaluating the effectiveness of the co-operation between staff and volunteers with open discussions of elements that do not work well can help your Early Years setting to improve its practice and management without having to depend on emergency measures.

CASE STUDY

Shipa feels passionate about breastfeeding and asked the midwife and health visitor whether she could help during the breast-feeding support drop-in in the children's centre. Her help was gratefully accepted as this is a very busy session and each mother often demands a considerable amount of the professionals' time. The three agreed what Shipa's role should be (this included setting up for the session and tidying the room afterwards) and she soon settled in. After a few weeks some parents mentioned to her that they would prefer the breast-feeding session to start and finish earlier so that they could get into the room earlier to set up for their play session. Motivated by her wish to help them, she agreed the new time arrangements with them and set up for the next breast-feeding session half an hour earlier.

FEEDBACK

Although Shipa acted with good intentions, she exceeded her responsibilities and made a commitment that was beyond her remit. Because she was seen by others as a representative of the breast-feeding group, they assumed it was appropriate for them to talk to her about their problems and to expect her to make a decision. It is difficult for you to influence how other people see volunteers in a group environment beyond promoting and being explicit about volunteer involvement. In this particular instance, it may be useful to work with Shipa to clarify the scope of her role and to develop her assertiveness so that she can respond to requests in different ways in the future. These are topics for a one-to-one discussion with her in the context of regular supervisions. This ongoing support for volunteers can prevent conflict and give the opportunity to use difficult situations as learning experiences.

Parents as employers

Early Years practitioners in committee-run pre-schools work in an environment where some of the parents are also their employers. In the private sector staff members may care for the child of the nursery owner, and in a nursery school a senior staff member may also have a child in the setting. These situations create difficult circumstances for Early Years practitioners as they may not feel able to challenge the parent who is also their employer or manager. This could potentially lead to staff accepting poor practice and not acting in the best interest of a child because of concerns over their own position in the setting.

Some difficulties arising from these situations can be limited by clarity of roles, for example an understanding that the pre-school leader, likely to be the Early Years Professional, is responsible for the curriculum and provision of care in the pre-school while committee members take the lead on financial and administrative matters. In pre-schools, especially those which have developed out of small local community groups, the drafting and agreeing of policies and procedures often seems unnecessary but developing clear guidelines while relationships are positive and constructive is less stressful and more effective than trying to deal with a crisis situation. Furthermore, the relationships between staff and committee should not just be based on individuals who work well together but be built on objective expectations which will still apply when other staff or committee members come into post. Similarly, the relationship between staff members and the owner of a private sector setting should be clearly defined and based on written guidelines.

When the differences and tensions arising from the relationships between employer/ parent on the one hand and employee/professional on the other are not addressed, they may escalate into conflict. This is sometimes aggravated because neither party clearly states what their expectations or their needs are. Using the committee chairperson's child in your setting as an example, you may have certain expectations regarding children's behaviour while the parent is happy to accept different standards of behaviour in her child. In order to avoid undermining the general behaviour expectations in your setting you will not be able to make an exception and will therefore have to work with the parent to achieve change. Obviously, you will have to adjust your approach according to the parent, his or her character, pre-existing knowledge and so on to find a sensitive way of addressing the issue but clear and unambiguous communication is the starting point. Conflict resolution which is trying to achieve positive outcomes can be broken down into three steps (Rodd, 2006):

Figure 7.1 Steps of conflict resolution

From asserting that there is a problem and a need for change you move to negotiating and mutually agreeing what should happen next. If the parent does not acknowledge the need for change and refuses to negotiate, you may want to try a problem-solving approach. This incorporates a collaborative approach based on the premise that if two people in the setting have a problem it is a problem for the whole setting. The problem-solving approach will enable the group to brainstorm, explore a range of options, and create 'win-win' situations without apportioning blame. The focus is on the problem rather than the people involved and the attitude is one of 'can-do' with a view to resolving the issue rather than strengthening or undermining the position of individual people. In our example the discussions could address general behaviour expectations in the setting, how valid the existing ones are, which ones may need amending, and which should be replaced. Occasionally, there are situations when the problem-solving approach does not lead to a resolution of the conflict in which case it may be necessary to consider mediation from a third party. A mediator may be able to enhance communication and mutual understanding and focus the different parties on the issues that need discussing rather than on individuals and personalities.

REFLECTIVE TASK

Consider a recent conflict situation you were involved in. What happened and how did you contribute to its resolution?

FEEDBACK

In order to resolve any conflict it is important to maintain effective communication between the different parties so they feel understood and respected. You may have employed some of the following strategies.

- *Use active listening.*

- *Look for and observe non-verbal cues and information.*

- *Help those involved to understand and define the problem.*

- *Allow feelings to be expressed.*

- *Look for alternative solutions.*

- *Encourage those involved in the conflict to work out how they will put an agreed solution in place.*

(Armstrong, 1994 cited in Rodd, 2006, p126)

Parents as friends and neighbours

Living in the community you work in will present specific problems, partly because parents do not always distinguish between you as the professional and you as the private individual. Reminding others about your different roles and explaining their implications is part of your responsibility as a professional. In a group of friends it may be tempting for a professional to talk in detail about some work-related issues but you have an obligation to your setting and to the colleagues and families you work with, and information of any kind should only be shared where and when it is necessary. The procedures of your setting regarding confidentiality and data sharing will provide you with guidelines where sensitive information is concerned. However, there are also concerns about sharing less sensitive, more general information as 'information is power', and knowing what others do not could be an advantage. In an Early Years setting where all families should be treated with respect and without favouritism not receiving information when others are may lead to resentment and create mistrust. Parents as well as colleagues may feel disempowered when others know more than they do. How information is shared within the staff team, with committee members and with families is an important question for a setting and should be clarified, potentially in a communications strategy which outlines how and when information is distributed to ensure that every family and every staff member is kept up to date and informed of all important matters relating to the children's development and to the whole setting.

Apart from professionals inadvertently sharing information when it is not appropriate, friends and neighbours may share information with you about others. This may pose ethical dilemmas for you, especially when the information relates to children in your setting. A number of questions will arise, for example: Is this true or just gossip? Have I observed anything to support or contradict this? What does this mean for the child in question? Is this something where I should take action? How will this influence my view of this family and consequently my work with them? The answers you give will largely depend on the exact circumstances and the nature of the information. Although much of what you hear may be irrelevant, it could still cloud your view of the family in question. It may be advisable to approach information received outside your work the same as information received at work: information of a sensitive nature should be treated as confidential; where there are concerns about the welfare of a child, appropriate action should be taken (for example, logging a concern or making a referral); concerns about boundaries or appropriate action on your part should be discussed with your supervisor or line-manager. Defining clear and strict guidelines regarding the boundary between the professional and the private is problematic because of the many variables involved. However, ongoing discussion of the issues is important to ensure professionals can work safely. You may want to provide staff members with regular opportunities to raise concerns or questions, for example in supervisory meetings, when you jointly agree appropriate action (see below for more details on staff supervisions).

When parents need help with parenting

We mentioned in previous chapters that Early Years practitioners often find the work with parents challenging, which could be based on the assumption that they understand it to mean talking to them when things are not going well. As an isolated incident, it is very difficult to find a sensitive and constructive way to discuss with a parent a problem their child may have. However, throughout this book we have developed an approach to working with parents which is based on partnership and mutual respect for each other's competence and which includes parents and professionals learning together to support the development and well-being of children. In the context of a collaborative approach to the well-being, learning and development of children, and an ethos of shared responsibility and joint learning, discussing behaviour problems or ineffective parenting strategies becomes less daunting.

PRACTICAL TASK

In the light of the different strategies and approaches to working in partnership with parents which you have explored in this book, consider what you could do to encourage a parent to change an aspect of their parenting behaviour.

FEEDBACK

You may consider some of the following.

- *Offer some information about managing children's behaviour and parenting skills to all families.*

- *Run a course which explores a range of common parenting problems which most families are likely to face at some stage with their child.*

- *Invite a relevant speaker to the next coffee morning.*

- *During your next one-to-one meeting share with the parent the behaviour you have observed in her child and invite the parent's views on it. Use her views and interpretations as the starting point for the discussion and the development of a joint approach.*

- *At the weekly drop-in initiate a general discussion amongst parents about the issue in question.*

- *Think about activities and groups outside your setting which may be helpful and support the family to access those.*

In an environment where the dialogue between parent and professional is encouraged and supported, it is easier for practitioners to raise concerns with parents, and parents will find it easier and less stigmatising to seek help. We know from earlier chapters how parents would like support to be delivered, but the initial response to parents voicing a concern can still be difficult. Parentline Plus suggests the following approach for professionals.

- *Listen to and hear what the parents and carers who come to them are saying, either directly or behind their words.*

- *Accept the feelings expressed and try to understand and reflect them back.*

- *Help parents and carers clarify and understand the dilemmas they face.*

- *Help parents and carers improve their skills, competence, knowledge and understanding.*

- *Enable parents and carers to take responsibility for areas that are within their scope and not to assume responsibility when it is not.*

- *Foster trust between parent and child, partner and partner and parent and professionals, and help to rebuild it when it has been lost.*

(Parentline Plus, 2004/05, p5)

As mentioned in relation to conflict resolution, active listening and acknowledging parents' feelings are vital. In addition, the emphasis should be on empowering the parent to search for and implement solutions to their problems so that they can stay in control of the situation and develop their parenting capacity. You may want to look back to Chapter 6 which covers adult learning for strategies to help parents enhance their parenting skills.

Parents will need support and encouragement during this process and practitioners will have to be able to dedicate some of their working time to the parent without affecting the care of the children in your setting.

When there are concerns about the safety and well-being of a child

When there are concerns about the safety and well-being of a child it can become difficult to maintain effective communications between Early Years Professional and parent. This is not the place to discuss safeguarding procedures and processes, these are explored extensively in other publications, but a brief look at how you can communicate effectively with parents in these circumstances is helpful. Regardless of the situation, that is to say whether a parent has made an allegation of inappropriate behaviour against an Early Years practitioner in your setting or a professional (who may or may not be related to your setting) has made an allegation against a parent, the parent is likely to experience a wide range of emotions: for example confusion, anger, disbelief, sadness, and frustration. Previously positive relationships will be strained and clouded by the concerns and allegations expressed even if the incident is not directly related to your setting, and Early Years practitioners will feel unsure about how to talk to parents about the safeguarding concerns or about other matters regarding their child. Recent research into communication skills for social workers echoes some of the approaches already mentioned in early chapters but also gives some further indication as to how Early Years practitioners can effectively talk to parents: show empathy, use open questions and reflections, and emphasise positives and strengths.

Showing empathy, an understanding and an acknowledgement of the feelings expressed by others, is crucial when communicating in difficult circumstances. Parents are often grateful for the opportunity to talk about their feelings, and having them acknowledged demonstrates your ongoing understanding of and interest in them and their child. When professionals show more empathy, parents share more information and are more willing to co-operate. When professionals use open, rather than closed questions, parents have more opportunity to express their feelings and their views of the situation which similarly will make them feel more respected and acknowledged. Reflections (summarising and saying back to the speaker what you understand him or her to say and feel) are a useful tool as they show that you have listened to what parents have said, and that you are trying to understand their feelings. Reflections will encourage the parent to explore the issues under discussion in more depth or you can use them as a way to move the discussion on to the next point. Even in difficult circumstances professionals should try to emphasise that, although there are concerns about the safety and well-being of a child there are positives too. Highlighting strengths and identifying what is going well can start the process of finding ways forward and making changes so that the situation for the child improves (Forrester *et al*, 2007).

Staff members involved in safeguarding children concerns may experience a similar range of emotions to parents: frustration, anxiety, disbelief, anger and so on. It is important to create a safe environment where they can express these emotions and talk about their concerns. This professional, confidential dialogue between manager and staff member normally takes place in supervisions where feelings can be explored, different approaches to problems discussed, and next steps agreed. In education settings supervisions are often used to review performance and progression towards targets but in relation to safeguarding concerns and more generally in the work with families, supervisions offer a space to reflect on how well you are developing relationships with parents, what concerns you have about their parenting skills, whether there are concerns about boundaries between your professional and your personal sphere, how you are emotionally responding to the demands parents are making and so on. It is particularly in challenging situations that the staff members need the dialogue and agreement with their managers to work safely and effectively. If you as the lead professional in your setting do not have a line manager to turn to, you may want to consider the option of external professional supervision. Although this may be seen as an additional expense, it will contribute to the safe working practices not just of yourself but of the whole setting.

Monitoring and evaluation

Apart from difficulties in the relationships with individual parents, there are also likely to be fluctuations in your relationships with parents in general. Small changes, like moving the parents' coffee morning to a different room, can have a ripple effect and lead to dissatisfaction and conflict. To be able to avoid or address problems as early as possible it is helpful to monitor attendance and use of services and regularly seek feedback from parents.

As mentioned before regular analysis of attendance data will alert you to families drifting away from your services and you may want to explore with the remaining families what the causes are. More importantly, you want to ask families no longer attending why they have stopped coming. This will show you which aspects of your service or of your relationship with parents may no longer meet parents' needs and what changes you could implement.

In addition to the more quantitative data from monitoring activities, evaluation projects will allow you to gather qualitative data with information on what families like or dislike about your services and how they think you could improve them. Evaluations can range from the very informal to the very formal, from post-it notes at the end of a session to a cost-effectiveness study carried out by an external consultant. There are good reasons for either as the weekly feedback from parents will alert you to smaller problems and issues and a bi-annual study will allow you to stand back from the daily work and see the overall progress of your setting. Regardless of the method, the use of the information and the findings is important. Having made comments parents are keen to know what is happening as a result and you may wish to share summaries and reports with them. Apart from informing your own practice, these can form the basis for a discussion between practitioners and parents to agree jointly whether any changes should be introduced. If parents know that they have the opportunity to express their views and that you will listen and respond to them, relationships will be more positive and collaborative and parents will feel more motivated to get involved in your setting.

Consider the different methods you use to seek feedback and evaluate your services. How effective are they and are there any others you could use?

The table below shows some evaluation methods you may be using including some strengths and weaknesses.

Table 7.1   Evaluation methods

Method	Strengths	Weaknesses
Feedback/ comments book	Allows for comments to be made as and when they arise, written open dialogue possible between parents and staff	Lack of confidentiality
Comments box	Confidential	Difficult to give a direct response or clarify the concern
Post-it notes at the end of a session	Immediate reflection on the activity	Lack of confidentiality
Annual questionnaire	Confidential, allows for considered response, gives overall picture rather than response to daily occurrences	Depends on good literacy skills, time-consuming collation of data required
Focus groups	Allows in depth discussion of a particular issue	Time-consuming; participants may influence each others' views
Interviews	Not dependent on literacy skills, can be carried out by bi-lingual staff to overcome language barriers	Interviewer may influence responses from interviewee
Monthly feedback form	Allows for ongoing review of an activity or project	Depends on literacy skills
Satisfaction survey by external agency	Objective assessment of your setting	Costly, parents may be reluctant to engage with strangers
Satisfaction survey carried out by parents	Sense of ownership by parents, possible to engage with parents who are reluctant to talk to professionals	Time-consuming to train and support parents

C   H   A   P   T   E   R   S   U   M   M   A   R   Y

In this chapter you have looked at different ways of overcoming difficulties in your relationships with parents and maintaining effective communications with them. It is normal that there are issues arising out of the different views, expectations and roles of parents, and practitioners in an Early Years setting; however, these do not necessarily have to lead to conflict or negative outcomes. In an environment which supports collaboration and partnership working, conflict can present an opportunity for reflection and learning which enables your Early Years setting to progress and provide better services to its families. By ensuring transparency and clarity of responsibilities and procedures and by fostering an ongoing dialogue between practitioners and parents difficulties can often be addressed before they escalate. However, when your relationships with parents become strained, there are a number of different communication tools which will enable you to continue the dialogue, including showing empathy, using active listening and reflections, emphasising strengths, and choosing open rather than closed questions. You can support the practitioners in your staff team to address difficulties in their relationships with parents by ensuring that sound supervision procedures are in place. Monitoring and evaluation activities also make valuable contributions as they enable you to identify difficulties and problems at an early stage and may suggest suitable solutions when partnerships get difficult.

Self-assessment questions

1 When you are trying to resolve a conflict and want to achieve positive outcomes, which steps could you take?

2 Which communication strategies can you use to communicate effectively with parents when there are concerns about the well-being and safety of their child?

Moving on

As already mentioned, details on how you can support parents to develop their parenting skills are in Chapter 6 – The learning partnership. To find further information on safeguarding children issues, you may want to contact your Local Safeguarding Children Board. By talking about parents and professionals as friends and neighbours in this chapter you have started broadening your reflections on families from the context of your Early Years setting to the wider community. In the next chapter you will consider the importance of the wider community for your setting and examine what impact your work with parents can have on their attitudes to and involvement in other community organisations and issues.

REFERENCES

Forrester, D, Kershaw, S, Moss, H and Hughes, L (2007), Communication skills in child protection: how do social workers talk to parents? in *Child and Family Social Work*, 13: 41–51.

Parentline Plus (2004/05) *Starting where parents are.* (Downloaded from **www.parentlineplusfor professionals.org.uk/cmsFiles/development_projects/Starting-where-parents-are200405.pdf** on 20 December 2008.)

Rodd, J (2006) *Leadership in early childhood*. Maidenhead: Open University Press.

FURTHER READING

Rodd, J (2006) *Leadership in early childhood*. Maidenhead: Open University Press.
Chapter 6 addresses conflict and potential approaches to its resolution in the context of Early Years settings.

Taylor, G (1999) *Managing conflict*. London: Directory of Social Change.
Explores conflict in the work place in an accessible, practical way.

USEFUL WEBSITES

www.parentingacademy.org
This is the website of the National Academy of Parenting Practitioners.

www.familyandparenting.org
Website of the Family and Parenting Institute offering a range of different research reports.

www.teachernet.gov.uk/wholeschool/familyandcommunity/workingwithparents
Although this website is mainly looking at school provision some of the information is of interest to pre-schools and nurseries as well.

8 Beyond the triangle

CHAPTER OBJECTIVES

After reading this chapter you should be able to:
- assess critically how parental involvement in Early Years settings can contribute to personal and community empowerment;
- analyse the role of the Early Years Professional in relation to the wider community and the empowerment of parents and communities;
- examine potential barriers to the involvement with the local community.

This chapter develops your knowledge and understanding of the community context in which Early Years settings operate and the role of Early Years Professionals in relation to these communities. The content is particularly relevant to 'S3', 'S30', 'S31', and 'S33' because these standards require you to reflect on your relationships with parents, on the range of factors influencing outcomes for children, and on your approach to working collaboratively inside and outside your setting. The areas of expertise of the Common Core of Skills and Knowledge for the Children's Workforce supported by this chapter are effective communication and engagement, and child and young person development. The chapter will lead you to a wider understanding of the value of your work beyond the benefits for individual children to the benefits for their communities.

Introduction

In the previous chapters you have explored the relationships in the triangle of parent, child, and Early Years Professional in great detail. However, neither you nor the child or his parents exist in isolation and your relationships with them are embedded in the context of your Early Years setting and the surrounding community. The families and staff members of your setting form a community in its own right with its own 'membership' rules, its specific purposes, its own customs and regulations, but this community is only a small element in the wider community in which a child grows up. As this wider community has a great influence on the life of a child, parents and Early Years practitioners cannot ignore it if they aim to enhance children's well-being, development and learning.

In this final chapter you will explore how parents and professionals can interact with the wider community for the benefit of the child. The strategies for parental involvement in your setting will be considered from the community development perspective and you will explore the parallels between your partnership work with parents and personal and community empowerment.

'It takes a village to raise a child'

This African proverb reflects how important the community is to the development of a child. Although the child herself only slowly expands her social circle from the immediate family to the extended family, then to friends and her first nursery or pre-school, and finally to her wider community, the people outside her family sphere have considerable influence on her world. Their culture sets the framework in which her parents raise her; this includes among other factors their religion, their values and beliefs, and their socio-economic situation. In a community which, for example, expects women to fulfil traditional gender roles, girls will be brought up to dress accordingly and play with gender-specific toys in preparation for this later role. Even if a family does not support the majority view in the surrounding community, it still shapes the child by leaving an impression of being different and not like others. In neighbourhoods with low literacy levels and poor educational experiences adults often do not value education and therefore offer little encouragement to their children to learn. Where whole estates have been out of work for a decade or more, children will grow up without seeing employment as the norm for an adult.

When the Government introduced Sure Start Local Programmes in the late 1990s to improve outcomes for children in less affluent areas it recognised the considerable influence the community has on a child's developmental path and her attainment at school. In addition to supporting Early Years education and childcare, health and family support work, Sure Start Local Programmes were therefore encouraged to work with and in their communities. By developing parents' confidence, increasing their skills levels, encouraging them to volunteer, and inviting them to become board members Local Programmes empowered parents to access services and get actively involved in the Programmes which in turn contributed to stronger communities with an increased capacity to improve their own environments. In addition, this empowerment had a positive impact on the children:

> *Empowered parents provide children with good role models. Parents have often developed skills for future employment and thus provide the children with a better future. Parents whose confidence has improved have better relationships with their children.*

> (Williams and Churchill, 2006, p9)

The commitment to personal empowerment and stronger communities continues in children's centres which are a key element in the Government's strategy to reduce child poverty. Children's centres are expected to engage with their local communities, for example by inviting representatives from different groups to join the advisory partnership board and by building on and developing existing voluntary community provision. Attempts to improve communities and enhance local democracy are evident in many other areas as well, for example, local authorities work with voluntary and community sector groups to meet local Early Years and childcare needs; in children's services young people contribute to the development of the local children's plan; and a Government White Paper explores the transfer of assets like village and neighbourhood centres to community management or ownership.

REFLECTIVE TASK

How are you as an individual involved in the community you live in? And in which way does your Early Years setting get involved in its local community?

Early Years Professionals in the community

A comprehensive approach to improving children's well-being, development and learning means an Early Years setting should become involved in its neighbourhood and wider community. This can take many different forms, depending on particular circumstances.

CASE STUDY

The pre-school sends a representative to the school's governing body. Through better links between pre-school and school it will be possible to prepare well for the children's transition from pre-school to school.

The nursery school governing body includes members of the local faith groups which will enable staff and governors to be more aware of the needs of minority groups.

Once a week two members from the local credit union run a drop-in session in the pre-school during the lunchtime period so that parents collecting children from morning session and those dropping off for the afternoon can access its savings scheme.

The pre-school works together with the after school club and the scout group to raise money for a new shared building which will provide a better physical environment for the children from the three groups.

FEEDBACK

These types of links with groups outside an Early Years setting are now common and generally regarded as being beneficial for the children and their families, for professionals and for their organisations. They help professionals to understand the needs and constraints of other organisations, while also leading to better joined-up services for families and easing the children's transitions from Early Years setting to school.

In some cases the need to get more involved in the local community develops when there is a threat to services; the toy library may be considered for closure because of a lack of funding or a local playing field may have to make way for new houses. In either case, facilities for families will be detrimentally affected and those with an interest in children and their well-being should be tempted into action. However, many professionals shrink from getting involved in issues beyond their immediate Early Years setting.

REFLECTIVE TASK

Consider why some Early Years practitioners may not get involved in wider community issues.

FEEDBACK

Here are some possible reasons.

- *They lack the time.*

- *They do not think it is part of their role.*

- *They fail to see the importance of it.*

- *They are reluctant to get involved in politics.*

- *They do not think that they can make a difference.*

- *They lack the confidence to speak up.*

- *They are concerned that they may be seen as troublemakers and create negative publicity for themselves and their setting.*

The relevance of the wider community for children cannot be dismissed; working with and within the community should therefore be part of the remit of every Early Years setting. Lack of time is a problem for many professionals regardless of their field of work, however, once we realise that something is important and is part of our role, there are often ways to find time and give attention to the matter concerned. The role individual Early Years practitioners play in a community-context can be understood to be the one of a champion or advocate for children. The pre-school representative attending the school's governing body will speak on behalf of the pre-school and its children to ensure their needs and rights are considered. Similarly, the Early Years Professional attending a local planning meeting to urge for a playground in the new housing development is championing the cause of children. The reluctance to get involved in politics may be understandable but this could lose valuable opportunities to enhance children's lives in your setting and in their neighbourhoods. In view of the fact that the Early Years sector has a very high profile at present due to the introduction of the Early Years Foundation Stage and the campaign to eradicate child poverty, it is difficult not to see the political dimension to the work of the Early Years Professional. Nurseries, pre-schools and children's centres are at the forefront of implementing Government policy including, for example, the extension of the entitlement to free Early Years education places to two-year olds and the related increase in hours. At the same time, Early Years Professionals have the opportunity to shape local and national policy by getting involved in organisations like the Pre-school Learning Alliance or the National Day Nursery Association which work and lobby on their behalf or by contributing to consultations at local, regional and national level.

Up to which extent individuals feel they can get involved in community activities or in championing the causes of children will depend on many factors including their under-standing of their own role as an Early Years practitioner and their level of confidence. You read earlier that some practitioners, especially those at the start of their career, may not have reached a level of professional maturity which will enable them to work colla-boratively with parents. This can be extended to the work in a wider community context: professionals need to feel confident in their roles to be able to work sensitively in partnership with others and meet the challenges this can bring. This confidence needs to be nurtured and developed in their setting based on an overall approach which values participation and partnership. Two of your key roles in leading practice in your setting will therefore be creating a supportive work ethos and empowering colleagues to become actively engaged in their setting and in the wider community.

Personal and community empowerment

Empowerment is an important concept in community development work. It can relate either to individuals or to communities and in general terms describes a *shift from a state of vulnerability or lack of power to enhanced power or control* (Williams, 2008, p63). As mentioned above there is a case for empowering practitioners in Early Years settings to be able to engage fully with the colleagues and parents but also with the wider community. Once they feel confident and able to contribute and influence their environment, they can facilitate the empowerment of parents. For both groups the empowerment of the individual:

> *refers to personal development of, say, self-esteem, confidence or feelings of self-worth that have been shaped or damaged by experiences of poverty, stigma or emotional deprivation. Empowerment of parents might involve personal development in the form of new awareness of their own strengths, assets, skills and resources to enhance their lives.*

> *Another form of personal empowerment refers to the notion of 'voice', that is, having a say in local service provision.*

(Williams, 2008, p63)

From the evaluation of the Sure Start Local Programmes we can see which factors or characteristics in a setting contribute to the empowerment of parents:

- being supportive and non-judgemental;
- being welcoming, friendly, informal, facilitative and respectful;
- valuing parents' own experience and knowledge;

- encouraging parents to 'voice' their needs;

- enabling parents to volunteer;

- offering training for parents;

- providing services and activities at a number of local sites;

- regular outreach to inform parents of services and opportunities;

- showing respect for and an interest in families' ethnic and cultural identities.

(Williams, 2008 and Williams and Churchill, 2006)

PRACTICAL TASK

In earlier chapters you have considered different factors which facilitate the initial engagement with and ongoing involvement of parents in your setting. Compare these with the factors above and evaluate the differences or similarities.

FEEDBACK

There is considerable overlap between the factors we identified for the successful involvement with parents and those supporting personal empowerment. In much of your partnership work with parents you are already empowering them – to become more confident, to be able to contribute to their children's learning, to change their perception of themselves and their roles as parents, or to contribute to the community in your setting.

Many of the values and principles you have indentified as supporting partnership working with parents also facilitate the empowerment of parents. Once parents feel more confident they are able to change how they engage with and support their children. However, their increased self-esteem and confidence can also reach beyond their families and they are more interested in the communities around them. Through the process of personal empowerment, communities can gain in confidence and be empowered:

> *. . . the empowerment of 'groups and communities' can take a progressive path:*

- *'Getting Together' – sharing support within friends and family leading to increased self-esteem, expanding networks.*

- *'Getting Involved' – getting and sharing/receiving more varied support, leading to new skills, meeting new people, confidence.*

- *'Getting Organised' – in actions which support the community – gaining in expertise and recognition.*

(Williams and Churchill, 2006, p4)

By coming together, sharing their problems and looking for solutions together, parents can exert considerable influence and effect change in their communities.

Take some time to imagine . . .

- *a neighbourhood that's 'supportive'*

- *a neighbourhood that 'shares its skills'*

- *a neighbourhood that works together to improve itself, and 'has fun' in the process!*

'Freedom Club TimeBank is an exciting new charity founded to help build that sort of neighbourhood' in and around Abbey ward, Cambridge, UK.

*We have the generous support of Sure Start Cambridge **www.surestart-cambridge. org.uk**.*

How does it work?

> *Many of us no longer live in the same towns and villages as our families and close friends. Many of us have never even met our neighbours!*

> *But we all have skills that are useful and valuable to other people. And they have skills that could help us out too.*

> *Freedom Club TimeBank makes it easy to share these skills within the community – making life better for everyone.*

What do I do?

> *It's simple. You deposit time in the TimeBank by giving practical help and support to others when it's needed.*

> *Then you withdraw time when you need something doing yourself by other members of the TimeBank.*

> > *(Freedom Club TimeBank 2006)*

The development of the Freedom Club TimeBank was initiated by a local parent who could see the needs in her community but felt unable to help her friends and neighbours as much as she would have liked. It was set up with the support of local parents and staff members from the Sure Start Local Programme and the Council for Voluntary Services. Feedback from members show that it is helping individuals to overcome isolation and make new friends, members are learning new skills, people from different sections of the community come together helping to overcome stereotypes and improving community cohesion. The local nursery has benefited from 'work days' when the garden was tidied and equipment repaired.

Before the development of the Freedom Club TimeBank the Sure Start Local Programme had already been working with and empowering parents for some time through its parent forum, the support for community-run groups, courses for parents, and volunteering opportunities. This provided the context in which parents were able to discuss their needs and identify a time bank as a solution to some of their problems.

Looking at the experience from the Sure Start Local Programmes a clear path emerges which leads from the initial engagement with families on their terms in their community through confidence and relationship building to personal development and empowerment. This leads to better outcomes for individual children in their families but the path still continues. Through personal empowerment, parents can overcome isolation and develop new networks leading to collective strength and empowerment to find a voice and seek joint action to enhance the facilities in their communities, making a difference to the environment in which all children grow up. This ties your work with individual parents into the wider context of the community and highlights its value in relation to community capacity and local democracy. Both practitioners and parents can actively work to enhance the environment for today's children but through role-modelling also contribute to the development of active, participating adults in the future.

CHAPTER SUMMARY

In this chapter you have looked beyond the immediate relationships you have with children and parents to reflect on your involvement with the wider community. Your role in respect of your setting's neighbourhood is a two-fold one. Firstly, you can assume an active role as a champion and advocate for the rights and interests of children either by routinely working with other groups in your community or by lobbying in relation to specific projects. Secondly, you have an important role to play in the empowerment of parents which enables them to develop their confidence and skills and to take part in self-help and other community activity. Engaging parents in your setting and working in a partnership of equals with them contributes to their empowerment. As a lead professional in your setting you will also be responsible for the empowerment of staff members. They have to feel confident, skilled and able to influence change before they can work with parents in empowering ways.

As a result of personal and community empowerment the environment in which children grow up can change. If parents feel more confident and are able to draw on wider support networks, the relationship with their children improves. Through their actions, individually and collectively, change can be brought about in their neighbourhood contributing to better facilities and services for children. At the same time as parents become participating citizens, they become positive role-models for their children and constructively shape their futures.

Self-assessment questions

1 Explain the impact empowered parents have on their children.

2 Explain the importance of empowering staff in the context of community empowerment.

Moving on

Many of the strategies for working with parents mentioned in this book are based on a community development approach; however, it is not possible to look in depth at community development work. You may want to explore this further partly by investigating the current Government approach to greater community participation and enhanced local democracy and partly by familiarising yourself with theories and practice in community work. Below are some suggestions for relevant further reading.

Freedom Club TimeBank (2006) (Downloaded from **www.fctb.org.uk** on 10 January 2009).

Williams, F (2008), Empowering parents, in Anning, A and Ball, M (eds) *Improving services for young children, from Sure Start to children's centres.* London: SAGE Publications Ltd. pp62–75.

Williams, F and Churchill, H (2006) *Empowering parents in Sure Start local programmes.* Nottingham: DfES Publications.

Barr, A and Hashagen, S (2000) *ABCD handbook – a framework for evaluating community development.* London: Community Development Foundation.
A clearly structured book which will help you understand community development. It has a very strong practical focus and will be useful to plan your approach to community development work in your setting.

www.communities.gov.uk
A website which gives details of the latest national Government initiates to enhance community life.

http://cdf.vbnlive.com/
This is the website of the Community Development Foundation which offers a range of resources, information and advice on community development and community groups.

www.timebanks.co.uk
A good starting point if you want to find out more about time banks.

Conclusion

In this book you have explored the many different aspects of working in partnership with parents in Early Years settings including its benefits, difficulties, and practical implications. The benefits of effective partnership working in Early Years settings are numerous for all involved. Parents gain a greater understanding of their children's learning and development while they also have the opportunity to develop their own confidence, overcome isolation, and learn new skills. Through the interaction with parents Early Years practitioners can learn more about the children they care for, deepen their understanding of theory in its practical application, and reflect on and enhance their own practice to meet the needs of families more comprehensively. However, the main beneficiary is the child as a more confident and more knowledgeable parent can provide a more stimulating and supportive home environment. At the same time, the practitioners caring for her in her Early Years setting will understand her needs better, and when parents and practitioners agree a joint approach she will have continuous care and support which will greatly enhance her well-being, development and learning. When practitioners engage with their communities and parents feel empowered to take active roles in their neighbourhoods, children will also benefit from better environments beyond their home and Early Years settings.

Throughout the book you have looked at the many barriers to working in partnership with parents but also explored strategies to overcome these. In many ways the effective work with parents is not a question of removing obstacles which is reactive but a question of proactively creating an environment where parents feel they can engage with professionals and which reflects the strong value base of your own practice and of your setting. An approach to parents and their children which is based on respect, genuine interest and curiosity about them will be helpful. Recognising that parents are equal partners in the nurturing and teaching of their children and believing in parents' and children's potential is equally important. Parents want professionals who listen to what they have to say and take their words into account when making decisions. This points to another underlying feature which influences strongly how effective your work with parents is going to be – effective communication and ongoing dialogue. Although this book has given many broad ideas of how to approach the work with parents, which strategies to apply with which groups and so on, it can only do that – give some ideas. What will work for you and for your parents will need to be discussed in your setting. You will have to seek the dialogue with colleagues and parents to learn what may be possible and achievable, how local and individual needs can be met successfully and how you can together bring about the change you would all like to see in the lives of the children. Through dialogue you can engage others in your vision for working with parents and assess how you can link the theory from this book to the practice in your setting. And by continuously seeking the dialogue with parents you will be able to judge how well your services meet their own and their children's needs.

I hope that your reflections while reading this book have given you many ideas of how you can extend your work with parents. As mentioned at the outset, working in partnership with parents is not as difficult or overwhelming as it may seem, on the contrary, it can be very exciting and stimulating – and it is one of the most effective things we can do to enhance the well-being, development and learning of children in Early Years settings.

Appendix 1: answers to self-assessment questions

Chapter 1

1. What do children gain from their parents' involvement in their Early Years setting?

   When parents get involved in their children's schools or Early Years settings, teachers have higher expectations for their children. This in turn enhances the children's levels of achievement. Children also gain because their parents' understanding of play and learning increases and they become more confident in their role as parents.

Chapter 2

1. Explain the importance of jointly held values and beliefs regarding the work with parents in an Early Years setting.

   If individual staff members base their work with parents on different values, parents and children will get mixed messages which may lead to confusion and uncertainty. There may also be scope for discrimination and injustice if there are different approaches and value systems within the setting.

Chapter 3

1. Outline the importance of early attachment between child and parent for the Early Years Professional.

   The early relationship between the child and her parent or primary caregiver forms the blueprint for later relationships and therefore has on influence on the relationship between Early Years practitioner and child. Furthermore, both the attachment between parent and child and the attachment between Early Years practitioner and child correlate to children's adjustment in school and therefore influence the child's educational attainments.

2. In the light of parents' comments about how they would like services to be delivered, how should professionals relate to and communicate with parents?

   Professionals should seek parents' views on matters that affect them and their families and take them into account when planning services. They should treat parents with respect and acknowledge their role and competence in the education of their children. The ethos of the relationship should be one of collaboration with a strong emphasis on open, honest and frequent communication.

Chapter 4

1. What are the main features of an effective parenting course?

Effective parenting courses link theory with practice and involve both parent and child, that is to say parents should be able to use newly-learned skills immediately or try out strategies that have been discussed as soon as possible. It should also be supported by clear and accessible course notes and material and be delivered by an experienced, well-trained staff member. The programme for the course should be well-structured and cohesive, and have clearly defined objectives while still having the scope to address parents' wider needs.

2. What are the main strengths and weaknesses of a parent forum which includes parents as well as staff members from the Early Years setting?

Strengths:

- Parents and staff members can develop better relationships in a more informal environment.

- There is better communication between parents and staff members.

- Parents gain a greater understanding of the setting and the issues concerning staff members.

Weaknesses:

- Parents may not feel able to speak up when there are too many staff members present.

- The Forum does not represent the parental view or voice.

- Staff members may dominate the meetings.

3. Explain the varying role of the Early Years practitioner on the continuum of access or process of engagement with services.

Making the initial contact: The practitioner has to meet the parents where they are, give them information on services and help them decide which ones are right for them.

Introduction to and take-up of a service: the practitioner encourages regular use of the service, helps the family to get to know other service users and ensures they can participate in all activities within the service. The practitioner also considers how the family could progress and develop by exploring with them the use of other services.

Autonomous and continuous take-up of services: the practitioner steps into the background and no longer needs to encourage or facilitate use of services but remains available to provide further information or other development opportunities.

Chapter 5

1. Explain how data collection can support your work with Black Minority Ethnic families.

   Data about your local community and the families using your services will help you to understand the home environment and the families children grow up in. You will be able to see the range of different faiths, beliefs and values represented and can plan your work accordingly. By comparing user data with community data you will be able to judge whether you reach all parts of your community or whether you need to target some groups specifically. Ongoing data collection and monitoring will alert you to changes in the ways in which families use your centre and potentially to problems within a family.

2. What are the main benefits and potential drawbacks of employing a staff member from a BME group to your Early Years team?

Benefits	Drawbacks
Easy access to information on the BME group.	Work with BME group may be seen as role for this one staff member alone.
Help with communication through translations or interpreting.	Fewer staff members make the effort to work across cultural or ethnic boundaries.
Increasing the general understanding of diversity and equality issues.	Unaddressed prejudices and stereotypes may make integration of the new staff member difficult.
Opportunity to offer culturally sensitive activities and events.	

3. What are the main factors which facilitate a father's involvement in their children's learning?

   The mother of the child is also strongly interested in the child's learning and development. The father lives with the child. If the father does not live with the child, it is helpful if he has a positive relationship with the mother. The Early Years setting explicitly invites and addresses the father. He is consulted about his views and preferences before activities are planned. Events or sessions are less discussion-based and offer more scope for joint activity with the child.

Chapter 6

1. What are the key characteristics of adult learners compared to young children as learners?

   - Their self-concept is further developed which means they see themselves as independent, self-directing personalities.

- They have considerable life experience which shapes their identities, thoughts and behaviours.

- They are motivated to learn by particular problems or dilemmas in their lives, often linked to changes in their social roles, rather than by learning to please others or achieve grades.

- Their learning is problem-based rather than subject-based, that is to say they want to find a solution to their particular dilemma rather than gain all the understanding and knowledge linked to a limited subject.

2. What are the benefits and challenges of having staff members with different learning styles working together?

Benefits	Challenges
Issues are explored more thoroughly in all their theoretical and practical aspects.	It may be difficult to reach agreement on the right course of action.
A more dynamic and stimulating environment as colleagues approach work differently.	If there is only one team member with a particular learning style, he or she may feel isolated or sidelined.
The team provides good checks-and-balances as theorists explore activists' actions etc.	There may be tension in the team if members do not understand their differences.

3. Explain the role of the Early Years Professional in relation to the learning partnership of parent, professional and child.

The Early Years Professional has a dual role. Firstly, she is a learner within the partnership directly engaging with parents and children learning from and with them. Secondly, she is the facilitator of the learning partnership for all colleagues and families in her setting. She shapes the framework and ethos in which this partnership is placed and encourages colleagues to actively engage in their own learning and support parents to learn (in addition to enhancing the children's learning).

Chapter 7

1. When you are trying to resolve a conflict and want to achieve positive outcomes, which steps could you take?

There are three steps:

Assertion   Negotiation   Problem-solving

When these fail, mediation is a further option. This involves inviting a third party to come and work with all parties involved to resolve the conflict.

2. Which communication strategies can you use to communicate effectively with parents when there are concerns about the well-being and safety of their child?

- Show empathy.

- Use open questions.

- Use reflections.

- Emphasise strengths and positives.

Chapter 8

1. Explain the impact empowered parents have on their children.

Empowered parents feel more confident in their roles as parents and generally have better relationships with their children. They present positive role-models to their children, and their individual or collective action can improve the environment in which children grow up.

2. Explain the importance of empowering staff members in the context of community empowerment.

Staff members have to work in an environment which respects and values them, be confident and clear about their roles and responsibilities, and believe that their contribution can make a difference to be able to empower parents and other members of the community. Their capacity to empower others is dependent on their own ability and freedom to act and express themselves.

Index